Another Day in Paradise

*Stories of transformation from the Camino
and other places*

EDDIE GILMORE

Brimstone Press

ACKNOWLEDGMENTS

Special thanks to Mark Lines who went through the manuscript meticulously and for both his helpful suggestions and his encouragement. Thanks as well to Laurie Green who I met 'by chance' at a monastery and who kindly introduced me to Brimstone Press; and for Mel Thompson of Brimstone who, like Laurie, gave lots of useful advice and assistance and was a pleasure to work with.

I am grateful to Angela, Hollyanne, Craig, Hanne, Liis, Phil, Peter, Henk, Gerry, John, Claire and Islay who all contributed a 'Pilgrim's tale,' and to all of the incredible people I have encountered on the pilgrim path. Finally, thanks to my most faithful companion on the way, my wonderful wife Yim Soon. I am looking forward to our next pilgrim journeys together.

ISBN: 978-1906 38594 1
First published by Brimstone Press
Copyright © 2024 Eddie Gilmore
All rights reserved.

http://brimstone-press.com
Brimstone Press is a not-for-profit
self-publishing cooperative.

CONTENTS

ABOUT THE AUTHOR

Eddie Gilmore grew up in an Irish family in Coventry and later moved to Canterbury where he was part of the L'Arche Kent community for twenty-eight years. It's where he met his wife Yim Soon and they have three grown up children. He spent the next seven years as CEO of a London-based charity called the Irish Chaplaincy whose main areas of work are with prisoners, Travellers and seniors.

Feeling that the time was right for another new challenge, he applied for and was selected as Leader/CEO of L'Arche Ireland, which involved moving to Kilkenny in November 2023. It seemed like a marriage made in heaven but it was not to be and he left in August 2024. He and Yim Soon saw it straight away as an opportunity... to walk! They will start with the 800 km of the Camino Francés in Spain. Next will be the 520 km of the Lycian Way along the Mediterranean coast of Turkey. That will be followed by the Via Francigena from Florence to Assisi and Rome.

As well as being a walker and a writer Eddie is a musician and has been most fortunate that in all his areas of work he has been able to share his love of walking, writing and singing! He has had the privilege of playing guitar to groups of Travellers in prison, to older Irish in care homes and to always-appreciative members of L'Arche communities. He has even played in an Alpine cave on top of a waterfall! He also enjoys doing regular reflections for BBC Radio 2's 'Pause for Thought.'

Another Day in Paradise is his third book.

INTRODUCTION

It was early in the morning and my friend James and I were on a bench outside a pilgrim hostel waiting for the water in the billycan to boil for our tea. The birds were starting to sing, there was the pleasant sound of rushing water from the river nearby, and the sun was rising above the trees. We were sitting there in companionable silence and then James said, "Another day in paradise."

I've walked now a few times on the Camino, the ancient pilgrimage route to Santiago de Compostela. I've been in other popular places of pilgrimage without necessarily having walked there. Each time I have met the most fascinating characters and heard the most incredible stories. I have come across remarkable connections and I have experienced little miracles; sometimes where I might least have expected it.

I've undergone as well some of the trials that have faced pilgrims through the ages: blisters, snorers, getting lost, getting wet, getting annoyed, the sheer physical exhaustion that can result from walking ridiculously long distances day after day while carrying a rucksack that digs into your back. Perhaps on top of that having to hunt for food and accommodation when you're at your lowest ebb. And yet with all of its challenges and hardships, and in an increasingly secular age, the Camino and other such pilgrimage routes are as popular as ever. I, and many others like me, keep going back for more. Why do we do it? And how does it change us and our perception of the world?

These questions have even piqued an interest in the public sphere. Books about long-distance walks reach the best-seller lists, and each year the BBC shows a three-part series called *The Pilgrimage*. A group of celebrities are brought together, rucksacks on backs, and they journey together over a few days to a holy place. They are from various religious traditions, or of no faith, and we see at first hand the ups and downs, both geographical and emotional, that they undergo. Each episode begins with the words, "Following a pilgrimage path, whether ancient or modern, can be a renewing and transformative experience." That has certainly been the case for me. It clearly is as well for those on the BBC show, and for some it is an intensely spiritual experience.

One of the key themes linking pilgrimage across the centuries is the place of story. Pilgrimage is usually a communal experience and as we see from Geoffrey Chaucer's *Canterbury Tales*, it is a place where interesting characters are encountered and where tales are told. Indeed there is something about the act of walking together for extended distances that brings people out of themselves and draws forth their story. Even if pilgrims in Chaucer's time would have travelled in groups for reasons of safety, the communality seems to be an essential part of the experience for most. I will tell some of my own stories from pilgrimage. And I offer a selection of stories from some of those colourful characters who have been my fellow pilgrims on the way.

The chapters are named after popular pilgrimage destinations, and I've been a pilgrim in each of those places myself. They are all from the Christian tradition, although many who walk are not religious at all. A whole three chapters are devoted to Santiago. The Camino, as the various pilgrimage routes to that city in the Northwest of Spain are known, has been a particular place for me, and for many, of transformation and encounter and miracles. It can be tough going at times, on pilgrimage as in life. But along the way there has been kindness, connection, laughter, singing, and even dancing. At times it really has been a little taste of paradise.

Come and walk with me…

CHAPTER 1

SANTIAGO (I)

Just like Chaucer's pilgrims setting off from the Tabard Inn in London, my journey on the Camino began in the month of April. The year before, my friend James in Australia announced that he would be walking to Santiago de Compostela as part of a year of celebrations leading up to his fiftieth birthday and he was inviting people from different parts of his life to join him for sections of the route. I knew one person who had been walking the Camino each summer in one-week chunks. Someone else had done it in one go over three months from Le Puy in France to mark her fiftieth birthday. It was something I'd vaguely thought I'd like to do one day and the letter from James gave me the impetus. I wrote back and said I would join him for ten days on one condition. I wanted to do the bit over the Pyrenees that I'd seen Martin Sheen do in the film *The Way*!

James agreed and we duly met up in the spring of 2015 in St-Jean-Pied-de-Port on the French side of the mountains. It is where many people begin the Camino and there is an office in this beautiful old border town where pilgrims can obtain their *credencial* or pilgrim passport. This document is stamped along the way and enables the holder to spend the night in the *albergues*, pilgrim hostels, en route. It is also presented in Santiago as proof of walking, in return for which pilgrims are given (at a small price!) a *Compostela* certificate with their name printed in Latin. The *credencial* originated in the Middle Ages as a kind of guarantee of 'safe passage' for pilgrims on their way to Santiago.

We set off on the first morning in high spirits but got lost on our way out of the town. I often say to people that getting lost is all

3

part of the pilgrimage experience! It is not actually easy to get lost on the Camino because the route is clearly marked by scallop shells and yellow arrows. We retraced our steps and found the (clearly marked) signpost adorned with a shell and a yellow arrow and soon we were going up and up. Due to our unplanned detour we met two women, Alexandra from Brazil, and Pina, a Venezuelan living in Miami. They had met one another in an *albergue* in St Jean and ended up walking all the way to Santiago together. It was the first of many wonderful encounters both with these and with countless others from a variety of countries and backgrounds, and each with their own story and reason for walking.

I was pleasantly surprised on the way up to come across a group of Koreans sitting and eating lunch. They seemed equally pleasantly surprised when I began to speak to them in Korean, and James and I were invited to share their food, the first of many shared international meals on the Camino. Also on our ascent, James and I stopped for what became a daily ritual for us, making tea! The day before I'd left for France, James had sent a message requesting that I bring a packet of real tea. He assured me he would organise everything else and he was true to his word. One of the best bits of advice I'd had prior to walking was to pack light. James had clearly not received this advice because he had in his (very large) rucksack a stove and a billycan. We developed a bit of a reputation for, amongst other things, being the two guys who used to stop at random places and make tea! It's quite normal in the outback apparently and, as said, it was a special ritual for us: a time to stop and take in the incredible views, to say a few psalms, and also to welcome others into that space.

We were on the Napoleon route over the mountains which had only just re-opened to walkers the week before and we were blessed with glorious sunshine and clear blue skies. This was where the great emperor had led his troops over the Pyrenees during the Peninsula Wars. It was also the preferred route of medieval pilgrims because on the alternative, low road there were lots of woods in which bandits might be lurking!

The top of the mountain is very exposed and can be fatal in adverse weather conditions. Indeed, in *The Way* it is where the son of

Martin Sheen loses his life, which is what prompts Sheen's character in the film to begin the walk to Santiago himself. He wants to discover, in part, what had prompted his son to undertake this pilgrimage. He meets a host of fascinating characters en route and he undergoes a kind of inner transformation, also a process of healing.

When James and I neared the summit, we were excited to find the remnants of snow, although the weather was so warm we were still able to wear shorts and T-shirts. The frontier itself was simply a cattle grid and having got across that in one piece we were now in Spain. And soon, having walked over twenty kilometres of constant uphill we were on the steep descent through the pine trees towards the village of Roncesvalles. It was whilst coming through those trees that I had my first meeting with a Korean couple who were to become long-time friends. Angela and Julio had given up their jobs and were taking some months to travel and to re-evaluate their life. Part of that was to walk the Camino, and Angela went on to write her own book about her experiences on the ancient route.

In the days to follow, whenever or wherever James and I stopped for our daily tea ceremony, Angela and Julio would just appear. We would drink tea and we would sing Taizé chants together, including some in Korean. It became a sacred ritual. I see this lovely couple whenever my wife Yim Soon and I are back in Korea and in the summer of 2022 it was a delight to meet up for a meal in Seoul and for the four of us to attend a Taizé prayer service nearby which, by happy chance, was taking place on that very evening. Angela presented me with copies of the two books she has written about the Camino, plus a large black and white photo of her and James and me in Pamplona taken in April 2015. The title of one of the books translates roughly as 'The strange country's Camino,' and a short extract is given below.

We had gone into a large restaurant in the town square. James had treated the four of us to an expensive meal and we had simply roared with laughter. The day after, I was chatting with a German mother and daughter, Daniella and Tina, who said they'd been in the same restaurant. "Oh, how did you know we were there?" I asked. "Vi could see you *and* vi could hear you," the mother exclaimed. Sadly, this couple had to abandon their pilgrimage shortly after Pamplona because the daughter was in excruciating pain due to ill-fitting boots and horrendous blisters. One of the Korean men I'd met on the way up the mountain on the first day didn't even make it to Pamplona, which is three days into the walk from St Jean. He ended up in hospital, having never quite recovered from those twenty-two kilometres of steep ascent.

...PILGRIMS' TALES...

In a Strange Country

We met Eddie and James again on the way from Roncesvalles and they asked if we'd like to have lunch together, so we gladly settled down with them on the nearby grass. The tea that James made was really good and the weather and scenery were great. Besides, both of them laughed out loud even though there wasn't anything especially funny, so it was a lively and enjoyable time as if they were out on a picnic. James said he prayed every day after lunch and had a Bible with him and we were happy to join in. I had a small Korean Bible in my rucksack and James suggested that we read alternately in English and Korean, and after that we meditated.

The moment of silence when you could clearly hear the wind and the birds was extremely peaceful. And we also sang some Taizé chants, with Eddie, James and my husband harmonising. It was very special. I couldn't have imagined a situation where a Korean couple and two old friends from England and Australia were sitting in a grassy field in rural Spain, singing the same song in their own languages.

We were given this time that we did not expect and did not prepare for at all and thanked each other over and over again. Later on, my husband and I spoke about that special moment: as soon as people are on this road their hearts are open and they are ready to experience anything.

In the *albergue* at Larrasoaña my husband took out the pasta and sausages he'd been carrying since the morning and made an enormous amount of food. There was more than enough for us and the two young Koreans Juhyeon and Heewon so we invited Spanish Gerrado, Italian Alessandro, and Japanese Nori to join us. Alessandro gave the pasta the thumbs up which put my husband in a good mood!

While we were eating, chatting and giggling a tubby man came in, put a bottle of champagne on the table, and disappeared without a word. The booklet I'd picked up earlier in the lobby had a story about the 'lively mayor of Larrasoaña' and I wondered if it might have been him. The champagne blew away the fatigue of the day.

Today I met nice people and received an unexpected gift. It was a day to be thankful for everything. Every day may not be like this but it made me look forward to whatever lay ahead of us.

Angela, South Korea

As Angela and Julio had discovered, the sharing of food and drink with the kind of colourful characters that Martin Sheen encountered in *The Way* and who Chaucer wrote about in *The Canterbury Tales* was a constant pleasure of the Camino and one which had continued for James and me on that first night in Roncesvalles. There was a pilgrim meal on offer and we ended up on a table with Toni from Spain, Elder from Brazil, neither of whom spoke any English (but which proved to be no obstacle whatsoever in terms of communication), and Zhu from Korea who was to become part of our little 'gang' of mainly Koreans and Italians. There was also Horatio from Mexico and a Chinese woman called Lee who spoke excellent English but who we never met again because she planned to get to Santiago as quickly as possible. Some people see the Camino as an endurance test and walk crazy distances day after day. I suppose there is no right or wrong reason to go on pilgrimage but I would advise people to not be in so much of a hurry that they miss the countless little miracles on the way or savour the incredible connections that one comes across, or simply the beautiful landscape. Another man on a mission to get to the end was John who had started his Camino in his native Holland. He always seemed a bit miserable and usually complained firstly that he had already walked 2,000 km, and secondly, about the large numbers of pilgrims on the latter sections, following the 'peaceful' stretch down through Belgium and France! I christened him 'Mr 2,000 km.'

At the end of our day's walking into Pamplona I had a first meeting with Anna as we made our way through the medieval battlements. She's an Italian who has lived for many years in Berlin. Her marriage had broken up and she had taken an extended leave of absence from work so as to take time out to walk the Camino and try to get her life together again. We shared a lot with each other in the ensuing days and, having kept in touch since, I can happily say that the Camino was the start of her healing process and that she has certainly got her life back on track subsequently.

The path to Pamplona had provided first encounters with various others that we came to know well. There were two Danes, Lars and Klaus, who were around the same age as James and I and with a similar sense of humour. Once they'd overcome their initial reluctance to talk to any other pilgrims we had some hilarious sessions together in the evenings. There was also Erika and Danella from Italy with whom we had lunch. It was the first of many meals, some cooked by 'the girls' themselves in the *albergue*s en route. We were joined on that initial occasion by another Italian, Giangia, who was walking with a guitar so he, I and Lily from the US gave an impromptu concert to passing pilgrims.

A day or two later I was happily walking along with James and with Angela and Julio when a woman sped by. Just when it seemed that she was out of sight she sort of magically reappeared (such little miracles, like people disappearing and reappearing, occur so frequently on the Camino that I came to almost expect them!). She was called Amelia and she was from South Africa. And just as she had magically reappeared, so there also appeared in the middle of nowhere a mobile van selling drinks, with some tables and chairs set out by the side of the path. Amelia invited me for a glass of wine. She explained that she'd been the recipient of an act of generosity the day before and felt she needed to "give something back to the universe." I said I'd have to pass on the wine, as earlier in the day I'd had rather a lot to drink at the famous *Fuente del vino*, fountain of wine, which is a tap giving free wine to pilgrims and kept in constant supply by some Benedictine monks. The Camino truly is the gift that keeps on giving! I let Amelia buy me a coffee and she was very pleased, as was I. She had a glass of wine herself, and why not? And there was some music playing so we even had a little dance, right there in the middle of a field by a pop-up drinks van next to a section of the Camino.

We arrived that evening at yet another stunning medieval town, this one called Los Arcos, and I was greeted wildly by a very special young American girl called Skye. She was walking with her mother Lesley and had something of the presence of an angel about her. This was swiftly followed by a round of cool beers bought by James then a second round provided by Lesley. And after that, James and I had a meal in a restaurant on the square with Pina and Alexandra and were joined by Amelia who insisted on paying; thus giving back even more to the universe. And then the five of us danced the night away. Another day on the Camino…

A few days into the walk I came alongside two elderly Spaniards who were making their way along steadily and cheerfully, propelled in part by their hiking sticks. One of them was called Rodrigo ("call me Rod"). In his fluent, if accented, English I was sure I could hear a bit of Irish in there and asked how he had learnt English. He explained that he'd been married to an Irish woman for forty years and that they lived in Ibiza. "Where in Ireland is your wife from?" I enquired. "Northern Ireland," he replied. "Where in the North?" "County Down." "Where in County Down?" "Newry." "Oh," I said, excitedly, "that's where my mum's from." I told him mum's maiden name, McStay, and he promised to make enquiries when he called his wife. They spoke on the phone every evening and her first question was always, "Did you meet any Irish people today on

9

the Camino?" I met Rod again the following day, for one rarely encounters people only once on the Camino, and he told me that his wife knew a Pat McStay who had been a butcher in Newry. "That's my Uncle Pat," I exclaimed. The next day, on the path leaving Estella, James and I had a rare chance to take a detour from the official route and thought, "why not?" Thanks to that detour we met a local man who was out walking his dog. I managed in my broken Spanish to explain the story of Rod and his wife and my Uncle Pat. He said to me, "*El mundo es un pañuelo*," the world is a handkerchief i.e. it's a small world. That became something of a mantra for me on the Camino; and off it, for that matter.

Some months later I was at a conference in London and got talking to a man called Rory whose dad was from Newry and who, on further investigation, also knew Uncle Pat. When I reported that back to mum she said, "Ah, sure the whole town knows Pat!" Then some years later I was visiting a school in London with a couple of others from the Irish Chaplaincy where I was working at the time and the deputy head was from Newry and it emerged that her mum had shortly before bumped into a couple of my aunties in a department store in the town. As I was to discover on the Camino, and many times subsequently, the world is indeed a handkerchief, and a beautiful one at that.

When James and I reached the small town of Nájera we booked into the municipal *albergue*, which contained a single, stuffy dormitory filled with enough bunk beds to accommodate 100 pilgrims. As I lay sleepless in my bottom bunk in the small hours, surrounded by a cacophony of wheezing, scratching and snoring and thinking that I might suffocate, I reached out to try and open a window. I was shocked when my wrist was grabbed by a seemingly disembodied hand from above, accompanied by some harsh words in Spanish. I swiftly retreated back into my sleeping-bag. I rose early, as did James, and we were sitting outside the hostel on a bench waiting for the water in the billycan to boil for our tea. It was a feast for the senses at that hour. The sound of rushing water from the river. The birds beginning to sing. The sun just starting to rise above the tall trees at the back of the hostel. We were sitting there happily not saying a word, and then James uttered the words, "Another day in paradise." After my return from that first stretch on the Camino I tried to say to myself each day when I woke up and opened the bedroom curtains, "Another day in paradise." It lasted for a few weeks, but besides the title of a book, it also inspired a song, 'El Camino.'

Nájera was memorable for another reason. Despite having good, comfortable boots I had somehow succumbed to that common irritant of pilgrims throughout the ages: blisters! But help is never far from hand on the Camino. Our Italian friend Danella had a little pack of needles and on that same bench outside the hostel she lanced and treated the offending articles on my feet. Before setting off the following year for my second stretch on the Camino I received what was the second most important piece of advice regarding long-distance hikes: two pairs of socks, one thin inner pair and thicker outer ones. Since doing this I am very happy and very fortunate to say that I have never again suffered from blisters.

After a few days James and I began to leave in the morning at different times. I liked to set off early and get an hour or two of walking under my belt before stopping at a café for breakfast. James would leave a bit later with Erika and Danella and the three of them ended up staying together all the way to Santiago. The walk from Nájera took me eventually into a village with a café where I stopped. The first person I met there was Masanori from Japan who I'd eaten breakfast with on a previous day, and who immediately offered me bananas and nuts. Such spontaneous acts of kindness were commonplace on the Camino and as I was nearing the end of my pilgrimage I was feeling quite overwhelmed with happiness. We sat outside on the pavement and greeted the pilgrims as they passed by. Eventually it was time to go in and get my customary *café con leche* and have something to eat. There was a CD playing pleasantly in the background, the final track of which was the lovely Italian song *Con Te Partiro*, whose English version is *Time to Say Goodbye*. Tears began to stream down my face. I felt that my heart could burst with gratitude for all the goodness I'd received on the Camino: the walking, the scenery, the encounters, the food, the laughter, even the tears.

11

As I sipped my coffee and ate my tostadas and tortilla, sitting with this kind Japanese man and enjoying together the music and the companionship, it seemed that life couldn't get much better. Such moments are fleeting, but no less precious because of that. We eventually had to leave to carry on walking. And when we did emerge from that cafe, who should arrive but Amelia, at a fast pace as usual, but she happily stopped so that I could buy *her* a coffee in return for her kindness on previous occasions. Then Pina and Alexandra turned up and there were kisses on the cheeks all round. And very soon after that, along came James and Erika and Danella. And we all just sat there outside that café in a tiny village in the North of Spain, where pilgrims have been passing for centuries, and we soaked up the goodness and the sacredness of that moment.

After nine days of walking we reached Belorado, from where I would take a bus to Bilbao and then fly home. I planned to walk one last day with the incredible people I had met and who had touched my heart. I would do most of the planned route for that day and then hike back to Belorado before leaving early the next morning. Anna wanted to walk with me one last time, also to treat me to breakfast at the hotel where she had stayed, the Quatro Cantones. As well as a restaurant it had a swimming pool in the garden and Anna had arranged for me to have a swim the evening before when she knew I'd been feeling out of sorts on arrival in Belorado. The swim was just what I'd needed.

On that final day on the Camino I'd risen at 6 a.m. in the municipal *albergue* where I'd spent the night. It was a curious old monastery building adjacent to the church and was a *donativo* hostel, which meant that you just paid a small donation and that included a help yourself breakfast (some of the *donativo* places also offered a shared evening meal, perhaps a time of prayer too). I made myself a cup of real black tea with milk and sat outside on the square listening to the sound of the river and to the singing of the birds. I was enraptured as a stork swooped down from its nest on top of the church tower. It was paradise indeed. After writing a couple of notes of farewell to people, I went to meet Anna and on entering her hotel I heard the pleasing and slightly otherworldly melodies of Enya coming from the restaurant. Like much else on the Camino, it just seemed sort of fitting and just what I needed at that moment. I told Anna about my dream of the previous night, my first remembered dream on the Camino and surely a significant one as I came to the end of my journey, at least for the time being. I was back in Korea and embracing Yim Soon's sisters, especially her eldest, and then also her mother; and I was in floods of tears, tears of pure joy. In reality I had not, at that point, been in Korea for fifteen years, and giving hugs is not part of the culture, and certainly not with ones mother-in-law! Anna was perceptive about people and situations and I could tell from the fascinating and in-depth conversations we'd had that she was knowledgeable about the workings of the 'inner world.' She said to me that I had received a blessing from the souls of these women. She added that I was receiving a blessing from God for a job well done.

We set off for that final walk together. It was a day of slow ascent, away from Belorado, past Villafranca and on and on and up and up to wonderful views across the valleys and to the snow-capped mountains beyond. We stopped eventually by a peace monument in a forest clearing. We were joined gradually by our Camino friends as they arrived in twos and threes. First on the scene were Zhu and Masanori and Guillerme, a Brazilian. Lars and Klaus strode in next, and they were followed by another couple of Koreans, Spanish Gerardo and his mum, and a German woman Cordula who was now walking with Mr 2,000 km, who had actually begun to look a bit more cheerful. Maybe love had come to him on the Camino! There also turned up a couple of young Korean women, one of whom is referred to rather enigmatically in my notes as 'the pretty one!' There was quite a crowd in the end who were gathered for my final meal and we all shared a feast of a lunch spread out on three picnic tables.

I hoped that I might also see Federika, another lovely Italian woman, to say goodbye. We'd walked together on one of the days for thirty kilometres and it had been such a wonderful encounter and indeed such a wonderful day, notwithstanding the developing blisters on both of my feet. We'd done the final stretch with Amelia, plus a new companion, Jan from Belgium, and the four of us had virtually collapsed into the first bar we came to. I had in there one of the coldest and best beers I will ever have and then Federika and I danced in the middle of the bar. Cordula had also been present and she told me later how she'd been touched by the sight of us dancing. I was informed by Anna on that last day that Federika had stayed in an *albergue* four kilometres further on from Belorado and had started off early, which meant that she would be ahead of us all day and that I wouldn't see her again. But who should appear suddenly at that picnic spot in the forest but Federika! "How did this miracle happen?" I asked her. She smiled and said, "It's the Camino!"

Lots of photos were taken and there was lots of laughter. It was sacred. A little bit surreal too when Guillerme asked if I liked Shakespeare. When I replied that I did, he proceeded to recite the whole of the opening monologue from *Richard III*! And then Federika asked what I would be taking away from the Camino. After a little thought I explained that I'd had an experience of deep joy and gratitude and connection; that my heart had been touched, and that I'd been able to touch the hearts of others; and that I could share a deep and special intimacy with those I met. And I added that my heart had already been full to overflowing after the first day or two, so that I had lived for over a week with an overflowing heart! I said that it was an amazing thing and that it was how I wished to live my life going forward. Guillerme, Mr Richard III, counselled me to write that all down so I didn't forget it, and thankfully I did.

It was time eventually for goodbyes (for as I'd heard in the café the day before, it was indeed 'Time to say goodbye'). One by one I said a final 'Buen Camino' to those wonderful people before they went the final few kilometres to the next town and the next *albergue*. The last farewells, in Danish, were with Lars and Klaus and there was one more wave to Anna and Federika before they disappeared out of view and then I set off on the long walk back. I realised later that I'd gone out 20 km which meant I had to trek 20 km back to Belorado, by the end of which my feet were in pieces. But it was worth it to be able to see more of my dear fellow pilgrims one last time. First there appeared coming up the hill Pina and a tearful

Alexandra. A little further on it was James and Erika and Danella. There was even an encounter at the bottom of the hill with Ben, a Frenchman who had been on the road, with his dog, for a year and four months! I couldn't imagine what state his feet must have been in.

Finally, I was delighted to come across Dadi and Jerome, who I'd first encountered in the early days. Dadi was a young French man who had got on the wrong side of the law through doing, as he explained to me, "*les bêtises*" (stupid things). As an alternative to prison he had been offered the chance to take part in a ground-breaking scheme which involved walking with a companion for three months. He agreed and had been assigned Jerome as his companion. This, then, was Jerome's 'job' for these three months, to spend twenty-four hours a day with Dadi walking extended pilgrimage routes across the length and breadth of Spain. I got the impression that Jerome may also in his past have got into a spot of bother but the experience was clearly transformative for them both and they had duly been welcomed into our motley entourage. Jerome explained to me at one point that Dadi had taken quite a liking to James and me (and we had certainly developed a big soft spot for him) and that he had wanted to buy us both a beer in the city of Logroño but that he hadn't been able to find us. I said how much I'd enjoyed meeting them and wished them "*Bonne chance.*"

The very last person I met on that walk was a new person, a French-Canadian called Steve, who enquired why I was going the wrong way, for it is highly unusual to be walking the Camino in the opposite direction. I sometimes wonder about the pilgrims in the centuries before mass public transport existed. Having walked for weeks or even months to reach their destination, and with their feet torn to shreds, did they then have to walk all the way back home? It seems that many people simply stayed at the end-point of the pilgrimage, whether that be Santiago or Jerusalem or wherever; and that often they would devote the rest of their lives to helping other pilgrims. Nowadays, nearly everybody takes a plane home from Santiago so Steve's question was a valid one. I happily explained that I had to leave the next day and had wanted to walk one final time with the wonderful people I had journeyed with and to say my goodbyes.

I stayed that last night at the Quatro Cantones where I'd begun the day with Anna, so I got a second swim on the Camino! It was strange to see a whole new wave of pilgrims arriving, and I mostly kept myself to myself on that final evening. After my dip in the pool I had a pleasant wander around the town, drank one last *café con leche*, went to Mass with the locals in the church on the square, had my final pilgrims menu meal. And I gave thanks. When I got home I wrote a song and made a video with images from my time on the Camino and posted it on Youtube so I could share it with my dear friends while they were still en route to Santiago. The lyrics are below and the chorus, inspired by that comment of James outside the *albergue* in Nájera, translates roughly as, 'Another day in paradise. To see the miraculous. To live like a pilgrim. In the life of love on the Camino.'

El Camino

We started walking from St-Jean-Pied-de-Port
We met two women, of them we'd see much more
The first of many great encounters on the Camino
Over the mountains from France and into Spain
In the feet was the beginning of the pain
And we soon discovered who could snore the most on the Camino

CHORUS

Un otro día en paraíso
Para ver el milagroso
A vivir como peregrino
En la vida de amor en el Camino

Guided by the yellow arrows and the shells
From old churches came the lovely sound of bells
It was almost as loud as the laughter on the Camino
Just when I needed it an angel came my way
With our Korean friends we liked to sing and pray
We shared our food and our stories on the Camino

16

Breakfast on the pavement, as pilgrims walked on by
So much joy in my heart that I could cry
Another day to greet the world on the Camino
The feet were sore but we had a lot of fun
We liked to sit and drink a beer in the sun
The simple pleasures of our life on the Camino

With all that walking the feet got worse and worse
I was saved in Nájera by a good Italian nurse
Giving and receiving acts of kindness on the Camino
So many moments of encounter every day
So many miracles and tender words to say
So much goodness to share on the Camino

I had to stop in Belorado
I went the last time with my friends and saw them go
They touched my heart, I wish them well on their Camino
In thankfulness I celebrate our life
And I'll return one day, and walk on with my wife
Sharing our love with who we meet on the Camino

*   *   *

I flew back to Bilbao in April 2016 to pick up where I'd left off twelve months before. The original plan, as mentioned in the song, had been for Yim Soon and me to continue together. In the event, she had decided to go to Korea to spend some time with her mum who was ill at the time so I went to Spain on my own. That was certainly a different experience to setting out with a companion. The whole experience was probably a bit less exuberant than the previous year but it turned out to be no less enjoyable. Just like on the first stretch I would get chatting with somebody when walking and then after a while move on and then maybe bump into them again two or three days later. And as with the first time there was a certain group of people with whom I would share food and drink and stories and laughter at the end of the day. Also as before, there was a profound depth of joy and encounter; and miracles, big and small, were to be found everywhere.

Those lovely little encounters began before I'd even left Bilbao. There was a bit of apprehension initially about being on my own, also the fear that it couldn't possibly be as good as it had been in 2015. I needn't have worried on either score. I had a few hours to wander the now-familiar streets of Bilbao before the bus to Belorado departed in the afternoon. I got chatting to a Senegalese man giving out leaflets who spoke to me in French. A bit later I got into conversation in a park with a one-legged old lady in a wheelchair called Verguña. The adventure had well and truly begun.

By late afternoon I was back in Belorado. I had a quick look at the town square and made a point of walking past the Quatro Cantones where I'd swum and had breakfast with Anna (and the day before leaving for Spain I'd sent a message to her and to a few others of the wonderful people I'd walked with the previous year). And then I was on my way again, following those yellow arrows and those shells; open to whatever or whomever the Camino would present to me.

It was four kilometres to the village of Tosantos, and I set off at a brisk pace, stopping only to change into shorts and T-Shirt. The weather was as warm and as dry as it had been the previous April. But it wasn't going to stay like that! I was headed for the *albergue* that Federika had stayed at and recommended to me, partly on account of there being a time of communal prayer in the evening. The *albergue* was dedicated to St Francis, Yim Soon's favourite saint; and it was a *donativo* hostel. As on previous occasions, that meant a shared evening meal and breakfast, in addition to a bed and the prayer time: all for a small donation. The evening meal was the usual bringing together of pilgrims from all countries and backgrounds, each with their unique story and their particular reason for walking the Camino. There was an almost festive atmosphere around the table, which was aided in part by the appearance of a couple of bottles of the local wine. Amongst the pleasant encounters was a first meeting with Brooks, a gentle and thoughtful pastor from Washington DC. After the meal I chatted with Santi, one of the two *hospitaleros*. They are the volunteers who sign up for a two-week stint to run the *albergue*s. They follow in the centuries-old tradition of walking a pilgrimage route themselves and then staying on to help other pilgrims. It's quite a business, I imagine, having to welcome a whole new group of people each day. He mentioned to me, interestingly, that he didn't always put the wine out in the evening but only when he got a good feeling about a group!

The pleasant encounters continued at breakfast. I was tickled to hear that Selina, a diminutive Chinese-Australian, had done holiday jobs in London and Belfast, working as an elf in Santa's grotto! I then had my first conversation in Korean on this second stage and, bizarrely, it was with a young American woman, Rachel, who had taught in Korea. I was pleased as well when Brooks asked me to walk with him. We set off together and had the first of many wide-ranging conversations. These often ended up with him talking about the increasingly abrasive and polarised political climate in his country, and his dismay about the possibility of a certain Donald Trump becoming president! Whenever I heard the news from the States in the ensuing years I often thought of Brooks.

My notes for that first day of walking include the line, 'A little unexpected glimpse of heaven towards the end of the day in this small sleepy village that hasn't got much apart from the church and the *albergue*.' There had been a pilgrim Mass in that church at 6 p.m. which was very moving, especially when we sang at the time of communion, and in the original Spanish, one of my favourite liturgical songs, 'Lord you have some to the lakeside.' As we left the church, a CD of Taizé music was playing. Taizé is an inter-denominational monastic community in the South of France and one of my favourite places in the world. In order to accommodate people of different countries and tongues they developed simple and repetitive chants in various languages, and these create a very meditative and prayerful atmosphere. It is some of those songs that James and I had sung each day with Angela and Julio the year before. When I returned to the church later in the evening, the Taizé CD was still playing and it was one of my favourite chants, and the one I'd sung to those assembled in the chapel of the *albergue* of St Francis the evening before, *Bonum est confidere in Dominum*, It is good to trust in the Lord.

On this second stage of the Camino I got into the routine of leaving the hostel early in the morning, sometimes when it was still dark, and walking for a couple of hours and delighting in the beautiful surroundings and in the rising of the sun. As I'd done the year before, I would stop at one of the many cafés en route for a well-earned breakfast: *café con leche*, a roll or croissant, sometimes a bit of paella. I would sit out on the pavement and watch as other pilgrims went by and I would greet those I recognised like long-lost friends. I loved the walking on the Camino but, just as I had done on that first stretch, I also relished the sitting outside cafés with my coffee and watching the world pass by.

There are ups and downs on the Camino, both in terms of landscape and in terms of mood, sometimes spectacularly so. A case in point was the walk to the city of Burgos. It was a second day of torrential rain and some of the Camino had been turned into a mud bath. The day had begun well enough. I'd had a peaceful night in a former monastic building in the village of San Juan de Ortega and after rising early I'd sat in the old cloister and enjoyed the sound of the rain as I did my morning prayer. I'd also had a comforting dream in which I was travelling in a car with a woman and asked if I could do something for her, also whether she could help me. This was to be borne out by events later in the day. I had a friendly exchange with Ingrid from Belgium as we were putting on our boots and looking out of the front door at a road which had been turned into a flowing river! And we were joined by an elderly and seasoned German pilgrim called Hans who took one glance at the bucketing rain and the water gushing past the door and said, "Well, we are here to suffer; we are not here to make party!" In fairness to Hans there is a long tradition of people who have viewed pilgrimage as a necessary means of suffering that has to be undergone in order to expiate their earthly sins and gain access more easily to their heavenly reward!

I had come prepared for the possibility of rain, for April weather in the North of Spain can go either way. I had waterproof coat, trousers and boots, plus a cover for my rucksack, but as any veteran hiker will know, heavy rain will manage somehow to find a way in. After leaving Ingrid and Hans at the *albergue* I walked alone for what seemed like hours through waterlogged woods. It must have been my longest solo stretch on the whole of the Camino. I eventually came to a village and found a shelter in which to stop and open up my rucksack to get out the meagre rations of bread and cheese I had with me. I was dismayed to find that the contents of the rucksack were partly sodden. There was not a soul to be seen anywhere and I felt miserable and quite alone in the world.

On previous days the Camino had been packed full of pilgrims. I walked another hour or two after that rather dispiriting lunch without seeing anyone. Where had they all gone? Had they conspired against me and taken the bus to Burgos? And then by some miracle (it's the Camino, after all) the rain eased and I saw the diminutive figure of a woman up ahead. I quickly caught up with Selina and it was so wonderful to see a friendly face. We walked and chatted until we reached the outskirts of Burgos. I was cold and hungry and decided to go into a café. Selina kept going, but gave me a recommendation of a place to stay for pilgrims which was slightly off the beaten track.

I had a pleasant interaction with the woman in the café who served me my *bocadillo*, a large and very welcome sandwich, and I sat and drank one of the best and hottest cups of tea I will have in my life. I was beginning to feel human again, and the process was completed in the most unexpected way. To my complete surprise the woman behind the counter asked me if I would translate for someone. "Who me?" I thought, "Why is she asking me?" I was duly introduced to a Swedish pilgrim called Sonia who explained to me in English that she had lost her phone on a bus an hour earlier. My task was to say that in Spanish to the café customers, some of whom were bus drivers. I must have made a half-decent job of it because those bus drivers were then on their phones to their colleagues in an attempt to locate Sonia's phone. My mood was transformed: thanks to those interactions with other people, and then the opportunity to help somebody. I felt like a new man as I left that café and strode down the main N-1 into the city. I had a little chat on the way with three Belgian women who I'd seen earlier but had not wanted to engage with, so wrapped up had I been at that point in my own misery. There was also a most enjoyable encounter with a woman in a fruit shop where I stopped to buy two oranges.

I finally arrived at the grand ex-seminary named Emmaus which was the place recommended by Selina and rang the bell. I was warmly welcomed by Marie-Noelle, an elderly French lady who seemed to be running the place single-handedly. After several nights in large and cramped dormitories I was struck by the wide staircases and high ceilings of the erstwhile training house for priests and I was luxuriating in the orderliness and cleanliness and in the sense of calm and quiet. Tea and a snack in the cosy lounge/dining-room was a particular treat, so too a long conversation with Marie-Noelle.

There were just five of us pilgrims there that night. Selina was in the women's room with two young Italians, Stephanie and Maria-Pilar. In the men's room I was joined by Arnaud, who was on his fiftieth day of walking, having set out from his hometown of Lyon. We spoke at length and he told me how he relished the simplicity of the life on pilgrimage. That was something that I valued too. You get up in the morning and pack all of your world into a rucksack and you walk; then you stop at night to sleep before packing and walking again. Thoughts turn to how far there is still to go, where the next meal is coming from, whether there will be a place to stay, how your feet are bearing up. As said already, the experience is not without its emotional highs and lows, but the usual worries and concerns of life seem to fade away.

Marie-Noelle initiated a time of prayer before the communal meal, so too a chance for each person to share a bit about themselves. It was a very intimate coming together of the six of us. Another of my strong memories of that stay was the lights coming on at 7 a.m. and going into the bathroom to the sound of celestial music which included 'Abide with me' in Spanish as I was brushing my teeth! It was altogether quite other-worldly, and I will be eternally grateful to Selina (who, like the vast majority pf pilgrims, I would never see or hear from again after the Camino) for telling me about that place and for her kindness and gentle companionship when I'd been at a low ebb.

I had also in the middle of the night taken the opportunity to wander round the lofty rooms of the building and to sit in an armchair at the top of the grand main staircase under a large lamp and read a bit about the origins of the Camino. I was half-way through my second stretch and realised that I didn't actually know what was special about Santiago! It was time to find out…

There is a guidebook written by John Brierley which is the English-speaking Bible on all things Camino. It was my faithful companion, with useful information about each day's routes and about *albergues* and places to eat along the way. He also provides some fascinating details about the background to the Camino. Although there is no hard historical fact, there is some anecdotal evidence to suggest that a few years after the death of Christ, James, one of the twelve apostles, sailed to Galicia in the Northwest of Spain and landed at Padrón or Finisterre. His mission was to preach the gospel to the pagan population in that region. The area around Finisterre was of rich spiritual significance within paganism, and James would have known that it was a place of Druidic ritual and initiation. This would have been one of many examples of the early Christian Church grafting its message onto pre-existing beliefs.

It appears that James met with little success and he went back to Jerusalem where he ended up getting beheaded by Kind Herod Agrippa in the year 42 A.D. This made him the first Christian martyr. It is thought that his body was brought back to Galicia by his disciples who wished to bury him at Finisterre. They are said to have sailed down the estuary towards Padrón; and in 2023 I was to find myself, with great excitement, on a boat following that very route. They met opposition, however, in the form of the legendary pagan Queen Lupa, who joined forces with the Romans stationed near Finisterre in an attempt to destroy the body of the saint. The disciples of James escaped by crossing the river Tambre, with the bridge collapsing just after they'd passed over it. Their reached Libredon (modern-day Santiago) and it was there that the body of St James was finally laid to rest.

The story picks up again in 813 with a shepherd called Pelayo being drawn to a 'bright light' or a star in a field. The word for field in Latin is *compos* and that for star is *stella*, from which we get

Compostela. The Spanish for St James is Sant Iago. Therefore we get the name of this famous pilgrimage destination, Santiago de Compostela. Other accounts suggest that the name may have come from the Latin word for burial *componere*, as there is evidence of a Roman cemetery on the spot, build over earlier Celtic remains. I rather prefer the first theory, with its echoes of the nativity story.

In any case, the local bishop, Theodomirus, took his opportunity and confirmed the discovery of the tomb of St James the Apostle. It coincided perfectly with the quest to reconquer Spain from the Moors who had in the early 8th century taken most of the territory on the Iberian Peninsula. The reconquest began with the mythical battle of Clavijo in 844 and continued until 1212 with the decisive victory at Las Navas de Tolosa. Throughout this period James was portrayed as *Santiago Matamoros*, Saint James the Moorslayer, a knight in shining armour beheading the moors with his sword. He also during this period became patron saint of Spain.

The first written record of a pilgrimage to Santiago is in 950 when Bishop Gotescalpo journeyed there. It must have grown in popularity in the century following that because in 1072 Alfonso VI abolished tolls for pilgrims travelling to Galicia via Val Carce which is near Pamplona. The importance of Santiago grew between the 12th and the 14th centuries with pilgrims coming from all over Europe. Its position as a place of pilgrimage surpassed even that of Rome, especially at a time when pilgrimage to Jerusalem was no longer possible due to the failure of the crusades. Reports of the miracles associated with the relics of St James also contributed to the growth in pilgrim numbers. Of significance as well was the instigation of Pope Calixtus II in the 12th century of the Compostelan Holy Years which brought with them certain privileges. Just as places like Canterbury would be packed with pilgrims in a Holy Year so too would Santiago see its fortunes rocket in such special years.

It was also in the 12th century that a French priest Aymeric Picaud walked to Santiago from a place close to St-Jean-Pied-de-Port and wrote in detail about his experiences. His five volumes were called the *Codex Calixtinus* in honour of the pope of the time. It was, in effect, the first travel guide to the Camino.

During this period a gentler image of St James emerged. Portrayed with his stick, Bible, scallop shell and wide-brimmed hat he was now referred to as *Santiago Peregrino*, St James the pilgrim. The scallop shell remains to this day as a symbol of the Camino. One way to spot pilgrims on the plane to Biarritz, near to St-Jean-Pied-de-Port, is the scallop shells hanging from their rucksacks! *Concha* is the Spanish word for scallop shell, which led to pilgrims to Santiago being known as *concheiros*. Pilgrims to Rome and Jerusalem also had their names: *romeros* and *palmers* respectively.

Various factors led to the subsequent decline of pilgrimage to Santiago. One was the Protestant Reformation in the 16th Century. In the same way that Henry VIII outlawed the veneration of holy relics in England, so too was pilgrimage frowned upon in continental Europe. There followed centuries of wars and revolutions, including in Spain, which would have made it highly dangerous to undertake any kind of long-distance walk. The long-term result was that by the 1980s there was just a handful of pilgrims each year who walked to Santiago. Its revival was thanks to a parish priest, Don Elías Valiña Sanpedro. He spent the last ten years of his life marking out clearly the Camino Francés (the French way) which remains the classic route to Santiago. By 2002, there were 50,000 people a year who were claiming in Santiago their *Compostela* certificate, having walked at least 100 km. In 2013, this number had reached 200,000 and included people from all over the world; and in the Holy Year of 2010 there were 250,000 pilgrims who arrived in Santiago. I'd been struck on my first time on the Camino how many Koreans there were. A common reason they gave for walking was that they needed time out from the fast-paced, workaholic culture of their country. Since the typical amount of annual leave in Korea is one week, many of those I met, Angela and Julio included, had needed to resign from their jobs in order to have the time needed to do the whole Camino.

I slept peacefully that night following my nocturnal reading and, as said already, was woken up at 7 a.m by piped music from the heavens; well, from Marie-Noelle's sound system at any rate! She organised as well a lovely shared breakfast. I left that wonderfully spacious former seminary refreshed in body and soul, and I was happy to linger for a bit in Burgos. I strolled over the river to the Cathedral square and found a nice café where I had a second breakfast of coffee and croissants and wrote some postcards. I had a feeling of deep joy. I even seemed to be on a roll with the Spanish, as I needed first to locate a post-box, then buy food to cook later. One especially fun encounter was with a couple of women in a shop where I wanted to buy a tin of tuna but couldn't remember the word in Spanish. It took a fair bit of miming of fish and the opening of an imaginary can and there was plenty of incomprehension but good-natured laughter until my evening meal was finally located on a shelf. The locals seemed touched that I was making an effort in their language.

On my way out of the town I stopped to take a photo of a tree in blossom and who should appear but Brooks. I was delighted to walk with him again and for us to share our adventures since we'd last been on the path together. On the way we picked up Rene from Holland, with whom we drank two coffees at the route's mid-point village. By the afternoon the sun was out and rain trousers had been replaced by shorts. The village of Hornillos eventually came into sight down in a valley and we found a fairly good *albergue* which mercifully had both washing-machine and dryer. Brooks kindly paid the three euros and four euros respectively whilst I did the cooking. It was tuna and sardines in tomato sauce with spaghetti, eaten out in the pleasant garden, with Brooks and I being joined by Karl-Heinz from Bavaria. Later in the evening as I went for a stroll up a farm track, luxuriating in the stillness and the coolness and the redness of the sky, I gave thanks for a day of almost countless blessings.

The blessings continued to flow the following day, although so too did the rain! I'd been out early in the morning, before the rain began, to watch a beautiful sunrise over the distant hills that we'd walked over the previous day. I'd slowly sipped a delicious cup of black coffee in the *albergue* garden, rejoicing in the sound of a cuckoo and to have 'another day in paradise.' I also had a little chat with 'we're not here to make party' Hans. I think I got him on a good moment!

The rain started soon into the walk and the waterproofs were back on for what became a long trudge along a very muddy Camino. But it didn't bother me at all. I was enjoying the vast landscape and it was comforting to see lots of other pilgrims, heads down and intent just on getting to the next shelter. We were all in it together. That next, very welcome, shelter came 10 km later in the form of a café in the village of Hontanas. The first person I spotted was Brooks who promptly bought me *café con leche* and a croissant. I also had a very happy reunion with Arnaud who was now on Day 52 from Lyon, and very tired…besides very wet!

I was glad to walk the second half with Brooks. By the time we reached the *albergue* at Castrojeriz the rain had stopped, the sun was shining and I had the absolute pleasure of being able to make a cup of tea with milk and then lying on a picnic bench in T-shirt and shorts. The simple pleasures of life! I had a first encounter with a Korean man who introduced himself in faltering English as Mr Park and who was a bit of an oddball (or so, to my shame, I labelled him). He sort of latched on to me and wanted us to go for a steep walk up to an old castle. I was a bit reluctant but decided to do it. Both the castle and the views of the surrounding countryside were stunning and I ended up enjoying getting to know this slightly eccentric man. Later on he joined Brooks and Karl Heinz and me for what turned into an uproariously fun evening. We began with a large beer in the main square, then went to Mass, from which we came out to see the most incredible rainbow in the sky. Mr Park was almost jumping up and down with excitement. Back on the main street we found a good place to have our ten euro pilgrim meal that was both very filling and very tasty. And right at the end, the patron appeared with a bottle of liquor and poured four generous shots for us on the house. A perfect end to an almost perfect day, but there was one further treat in store. Back at the *albergue*, the Italians Stephanie and Maria-Pilar had arrived, and just as with Arnaud earlier in the day, we greeted one another like long lost friends.

Frómista was the next stopping place along the way and I decided to have a break from the municipal *albergue*s and book into a private room. That was one of the best twenty euros I'll ever spend! I was tired after an almost sleepless night in Castrojeriz and an exhilarating but tough day of walking. It began with what looked from the bottom like an almost vertical piece of climbing up the Alto de Mostelares, which culminated at its 900-metre peak. It was like being in heaven and looking down upon the earth. On the descent I got chatting to Danielle from Slovakia who was to become part of my little Camino Stage 2 gang!

Despite the good, strenuous exercise of the day, I was feeling a bit sorry for myself as I reached Frómista and checked into my solitary room. I wrote a postcard to Yim Soon in an attempt to cheer myself up and went in search of a shop to buy a stamp. On the way I met a father and daughter from the States, Dave and Hollyanne (and her story is told below). I explained what I was doing and Hollyanne promptly reached into her bag and presented me with a stamp. It was a small act of kindness but it meant the world to me at that moment. Several years later I was exchanging messages with Hollyanne on Facebook and I said that I'd never forget her gift of a stamp: just when I really needed a stamp, and just when I needed a bit of kindness and connection.

…PILGRIMS' TALES…

Delta

At the Chrysler Museum of Art in Norfolk, Virginia, where I went to college, there's a painting on display called 'The Neophyte' by Gustave Doré. It features a young man at a monastery who has just taken his vows. He regrets them and he feels trapped. When I was in college I also felt trapped. I was a frequent visitor to this museum and I would spend countless moments looking at this painting marvelling at how I had the same feeling of longing to escape; not from religion, but from the confinement of my circumstances. Religion set me free. College didn't.

I came home from school one November day in 2015 and my parents proposed that I hike the Camino. I believe I agreed before they finished explaining it to me. As a twenty-year-old, college terrified me. Accepting the offer to walk the Camino with my father is the single most transformative decision I've made in my life so far.

May 9, 2016: We sat around a table at the last *albergue* before we reached Santiago de Compostela. There were quiet giggles and sighs of acceptance that it was coming to an end. Some of us had been together from the start, others had joined just days before. As I sat in the company of people who had been no more than strangers four weeks prior, I realized they were now a cornerstone of this part of my life.

I recall sitting silently and observing every fine detail: the Australian accent, tattoos on a hand, the musk of a German, and the presence of my father. I wondered how all those we had met over the last four weeks would have fitted into this scene. Through my hazed eyes, thanks to the wine, I desperately desired to remember the most unnecessary detail so insignificant to Father Time, but priceless to me.

The quiet clatter of side conversations begged for my listening ear while my eyes darted from face to face cementing them in my memory. We were weary from walking, the Spanish sun, wet boots, unbearable beds, blisters, heavy packs, and sweat-stained clothes. An unspoken expectation of putting off sleep for as long as achievable was understood by us that night. We were tragically aware that we would never find ourselves in this precise situation ever again. After we reached Santiago, we would all be forced in different directions, to our homes. A solemn cloud of dread for the coming morning floated over us that night. When the wine was gone and our limits reached, we finally retired to bed. The next morning brought with it a rainy start to the end of an era.

When you interact with something as ancient as the Camino, it is woven into your identity and it becomes the window through which you observe the world. There isn't a single thing you can do to remove it from your essence.

Now, more than seven years later, I am still painstakingly

beguiled by the Camino. This is immutable. I am incapable of believing there is another cultural experience that can satiate in the same way my perennial desire for travel and human connection

Hollyanne, USA

(NB The title of this piece has a three-fold meaning for Hollyanne. Firstly, a delta is a place where a river splits into different sections, just as pilgrims on the Camino share one path for a short time before they must part ways. Secondly, change in mathematics can be denoted by the uppercase Greek letter delta, and the Camino changes the way we relate to others and the world. Finally, it's the name of one of her favourite songs by *Mumford & Sons*!)

After posting my card in Frómista, who should appear but Mr Park and we went together to the pilgrims Mass in the church. I enjoyed seeing lots of my fellow *peregrinos*, and there was a first meeting with Brad, a high school Maths teacher from Seattle. He was great company and, like Danielle from earlier, he was also to end up in my gang! Indeed, he ended up walking with Brooks all the way to Santiago.

I felt like a new man when I awoke the following morning in my own room and took a shower in my own little bathroom. Having one night off from the throng in the municipal *albergue* had been a shrewd move and there was a spring in my step as I set out early on that day's 20 km hike to Carrión. On the way out of the town I met a young Korean woman Soyeon and we chatted easily as we strode along the *senda*. These are long, straight paths that often run alongside roads. We were well and truly into that section of the Camino known as the *meseta*, the prairie: flat, largely treeless, with few towns and villages and, I can imagine, pretty brutal in the full heat of summer. When a friend of mine, Annette did the Camino she opted to leave out that whole section and caught a train from Burgos to León, where she re-commenced the walk! I didn't really mind it. The temperature in April was pleasant, the rain had finally stopped, and I got into conversation easily with people, like a lovely young German couple, Philipp and Anni. It was their first holiday together and they seemed touched that I was taking an interest in them. As we made our way along the *senda*, I was equally touched to hear a bit of their story and before I knew it we were entering the historic old town of Carrión, which is famous on the Camino as being the place of the singing nuns!

I made straight for Santa Maria, the convent of said nuns, and was welcomed like the Prodigal Son by a Korean sister, who was overjoyed when I greeted her in her native tongue. After laying claim to a bunk bed in one of the dormitories there was time to do a bit of washing and to have a beer with Brooks who had also come in search of the singing nuns. There followed one of the most uplifting and fun evenings of my life. There was Vespers, evening prayer, with the sisters in their chapel, then an hour of singing and of the sizeable group of pilgrims introducing themselves. A German sister led the songs on her guitar and when I asked if I could do one, she gladly handed it over. I sang the song I'd written a year earlier after my first stage, 'El Camino', and I was filmed doing so on a range of phones! Stephanie and Maria-Pilar were part of that group and when I bumped into them a couple of days later I was immensely touched when Maria-Pilar told me that she'd been singing the chorus of the song ever since, 'Un otro día en paraiso, para ver el milagroso.'

Mass followed that wonderful hour of songs and stories, then a big session of communal cooking and eating. It had truly been another day in paradise, from start to finish.

The next day was rather special too! I left Santa Maria at 6.30 a.m. and was happy to be out in the dark but couldn't find the bakery, despite the enticing smell of fresh bread. I found it eventually and was first in the queue when it opened at 7. The second in the queue: Mr Park! The purchase of a demi-baguette was essential because there would be no shop or café, no anything, for 17 km.

I set out in the cool of the early morning along the long, straight, flat gravel path that follows the old Roman road, the Via Aquitania. It was good to walk alone for a while, although I was equally happy to catch up with two Korean-Canadian brothers, Eric and Logan and we shared food in a rare bit of shade. Later on that long, long

31

stretch I encountered Jesús from Madrid who told me that he'd hardly spoken to anyone in days because he didn't speak any English and none of the pilgrims he'd met had spoken Spanish! I asked him why he'd decided to come on the Camino and he explained to me that his day-to-day life had fallen into the same routine of, "*Casa, garaje, coche, trabajo, cerveza!*" 'Home, garage, car, work, beer." Each summer too he went with his wife and daughter to exactly the same place on holiday. This year, he said, he simply needed something different.

Learning foreign languages can be hard work and as a native English-speaker there might not even seem to be any need to put yourself through the bother. Following my exchange with Jesús, his first conversation for a few days in his own country, I saw that working on my Spanish in advance of the Camino had been so, so worth it. And I'll never, ever forget the plaintive reciting of his daily routine: *casa, garaje, coche, trabajo, cerveza…* I hope that he manged to find something different on the Camino, or that he was able to return to that routine with greater peace and acceptance.

We eventually reached the café at Calzadilla. Jesús kept going and I stopped and bought a cup of tea and sat outside to greet a variety of pilgrims, known and unknown. After my Spanish triumph with Jesús, I even got to speak my first Danish of Stage II. Richard was a Dane who lived in a town called Sorø, near which I had once spent a year and from where I used to catch the train to Copenhagen. I also encountered Brooks at the café and we walked together for the last stretch to Terradillos. There we found a nice *albergue*, and had beer and ice cream on the terrace in the warm afternoon sun to keep us going till the ten euro three-course (including wine) pilgrim menu. Just before that culinary treat there was time to lie down in the grass, and I felt all the goodness of those days, like the sunshine, seeping into and enveloping me.

On the following day's walk to Bercianos I stopped in a square in the pretty old town of Sahagún and sat at a shaded café table where I had some time to allow the experiences of the preceding days to sink in a bit. I'd had the unexpected gift of my own room in the *albergue* at Terradillos so had managed to get a decent night's sleep. I'd also left in the dark at 6 o'clock. It was rather magical to be walking at that hour, with a big, clear moon and shining stars to guide my way along the dirt track. I turned periodically to revel in the rising sun behind me, and I didn't mind that neither of the cafés en route were open. It was simply too early! I pressed on and reached Sahagún at nine o'clock.

As I sat outside the café with my (very well-earned) breakfast I reflected on how deeply blessed I had been on that second stage of the Camino. As with the first stage I had found a wonderful, international bunch of fellow pilgrims with whom to walk and talk and eat and drink and laugh; besides the sharing of encouraging words and little acts of kindness. How my heart had been touched; and how, it appeared, I had been able to touch others. I was also immensely grateful for my family and friends, who I held in my prayer each day.

Bercianos del Real Camino is one of many villages in the North of Spain whose economic fortunes have been transformed by the pilgrim trade. There was a fairly large *donativo albergue*, beloved of pilgrims like myself since it provides a communal evening meal and even breakfast; and all for a small donation. As explained already, such places are run for two-week stints by *hospitaleros*, usually people who have walked the Camino themselves. Their job, as the name suggests, is hospitality, and Fernando and Mario, our *hospitaleros* at Bercianos, did their job extremely well. There was a feast of a meal, including wine, with everyone sat at long benches. I imagined it must have been a not dissimilar scene to that in a Middle Ages hostel on the Pilgrims Way to Canterbury. The icing on the cake that evening was going out with Mexican Orlando to a bar to watch the football! Fernando and Mario had kindly agreed to let us back in after 10 p.m., the curfew hour!

It was a fairly sleepless night because Orlando who was in my room turned out to be a snorer and another of my roommates, American Bill, was a cougher! He was subsequent referred by me to fellow pilgrims as 'coughing Bill', together with a warning not to end up sharing a room with him! It didn't affect my mood, and I enjoyed the breakfast of hot chocolate and bread. There were good memories for me of the breakfasts at Taizé, the monastic community in France that I've visited several times. As explained earlier, the place is famous in some circles for its Taizé chants, which are short and repetitive, in a variety of languages and very meditative. Many people come and spend a week there, and the community calls these weeks 'A pilgrimage of trust on Earth.'

I was one of the last to leave the *albergue* at Bercianos and there was a most touching farewell with Fernando and Mario. They would have a few hours to clean up the house and then they would be welcoming a completely new group of people. I was on the road for the second last time on my Camino Stage 2. I walked with Dean from Ireland until the first café where I had my customary *café con leche* before setting off again and catching up with Shirley and Ron from Melbourne for a quick exchange. I was happy then to be on my own and didn't mind that the long, straight path followed a long, straight road! I was delighted to meet some, by now, old faces in the walled town of Mansilla de las Mullas. These included Brooks and Brad, also Steve and Darlene from Canada who had always been most generous with me in the sharing of food along the way. We found a bar and drank beer and how we laughed! There was a bit of gentle teasing of Brooks for his use of 'Jacotrans,' a service whereby ones rucksack is transported, for a small price, to the next destination. "I'm not sure what they'll say in Santiago, Brooks, when they hear you didn't carry your rucksack!" was one of the comments made. Brooks took it all in good grace, as we ordered another round of beers.

There were no coughers in my room that night, rather some of those wonderful people who had touched my heart on this second stint on the Camino. There was Brad and Brooks, plus Slovakian Danielle, and Nicola, the anime afficionado from Berlin. I was delighted to see other familiar faces at that, the municipal *albergue*: the Italians, Maria Pilar and Stephanie, Matt from Nebraska; so too Steve and Darlene and Orlando. Earlier on, Brad and I had gone to the supermarket to buy the ingredients for a last communal meal, and Selina had helped us carry the bags back to the *albergue*. I had directed a large, international and enthusiastic group of pilgrims in the kitchen in the making of tomato sauce and pasta, which went down very well with the bottles of local red wine that Brad had contributed. The group included a couple of young

34

German women who were a bit shy and had kept pretty much to themselves on the Camino until then but who seemed delighted to be part of this joyful banquet.

It was an easy, final 19 km day of walking. I left Mansilla via the long, medieval bridge and followed the pathway by the road to León. There were more good conversations en route: with Brad and Brooks, and with three women who were all called Kathy! The three Kathys! You meet them all on the Camino! I was excited to come across a church dedicated to St Thomas of Canterbury. Brooks and I went in for a pray and discovered that it was in fact a museum and a welcome point for pilgrims and we chatted a bit with the man running the place.

As we crossed the long footbridge over the river into León we caught up again with Brad and it was fitting for the three of us to enter that old Roman town together. The name of the city is derived from the word for legion as it was a key Roman garrison, and with its narrow, twisting lanes and large open spaces and old houses and churches, not to mention the old medieval walls, it's stunningly beautiful. It's also something of a party town for pilgrims! But before the party started for me I wanted to find where I was staying. There were several choices on offer. I went for Santa Maria, partly as it's run by a community of sisters who would be having an evening prayer that pilgrims could join. Danielle and Nicola had made the same call and we were pleased to be given a little plate of spaghetti on arrival. I followed that with a glass of peppermint tea in the quiet cloistered garden and a bit of a nap in the sun. And then I was ready to party.

I wandered slowly and contentedly back towards the centre of León and kept on meeting familiar faces from my ten days of walking. There was Dan and John from Los Angeles, Un Bin from Korea, the German couple, Philipp and Anni, and Japanese Kasumi who needed food and who I sent off with a local woman to the nearest supermarket. There was a joyful reunion with four retired people, two couples, from the Northeast of France whom I had dubbed 'the Alsace four.' They had always loved to practise their, fairly limited, English on me, using certain phrases which will be well known to a certain generation of French from their schooldays: 'Where is Brian?' 'Brian is in the kitchen.' Whenever I'd seen them on the way I used to call out, "Where is Brian?" and one of them would shout out delightedly, "ee is een ze keechen!" I was incredibly touched when one of the four, Jean-Denis commented that his image of me on the Camino was of a locomotive pulling people along. He also asked what I would take back with me. My reply: "A heart full of goodness and blessings and joy."

The main street leading to the cathedral was heaving and on a long table outside one of the many bars and restaurants there was a large group of hard-drinking pilgrims. There was Dean and two other Irish guys, there was a big-bearded bear of a man from Alabama, there was Klaus from Denmark who was happy to chat a bit in Danish with me, and there was Stephanie who had been born in Hinkley and later move to New Zealand and whose accent was a curious mix of English Midlands and Kiwi. I'd first spoken to her at the café at the end of the interminable 17 km along the bare, flat *senda*. There was Hollyanne (who had given me the stamp) and her dad Dave who were chatting with Brad, plus the German girls, Vicky and Julia, whose shyness had by now completely evaporated. The party was in full swing and I was happy to spend some time there greeting pilgrims old and new before exploring a bit more of the city beyond the Cathedral Square. I was back at the Cathedral a bit later, the rendezvous point of my little Camino Stage 2 gang. There was Brad and Brooks and Orlando and Nicola and me, and we were joined by Lasse from Copenhagen who I was excited to hear had helped Lucas Graham with the writing of the hit song '7 Years.' Our final meal together was a pizza, and we were back at Santa Maria in time for Compline, night prayer, and a blessing from the sisters. My Camino Stage 2 was indeed complete.

I had an early breakfast in the *albergue* with Selina, Danielle and Nicola and there were some touching goodbyes as well with Stephanie and Maria-Pilar. And from there I walked back across the river but this time to the station to catch my train to Madrid and then the plane back home. I would be back the following year for the final stretch to Santiago, and that time I would definitely have my wonderful wife with me.

CHAPTER 2

SANTIAGO (II)

Yim Soon and I arrived in León in October 2017 for what was to be my third and final stage of the Camino Francés to Santiago. Our youngest child had just flown the nest and it was the month before our twenty-fifth wedding anniversary so walking the Camino together was a special way to celebrate our marriage and to mark a major transition point in our life. We spent the first night in Santa Maria where I'd finished off the previous April. I was pleased to discover that it still cost just ten euros including breakfast, plus a snack on arrival, plus the chance to join the sisters in the evening for Compline and a blessing.

It was still dark when we set off out of the city on that first day of walking and we almost immediately got chatting to a couple from New York, Nancy and Tim, with whom we would share several conversations and meals. We also had a first encounter with Ariel from Brazil. An interesting German-style *albergue* awaited us in Hospital de Órbigo, and we went out with Nancy and Tim for a pilgrims' meal and a traditional music concert in the village hall. Our Camino had got off to a promising start.

There was a first meeting the following day in the high hills with Agnieszka from Poland. Like Amelia from my first time on the Camino, Agnieszka was travelling at great pace, explaining that she was trying to get to the noon Mass in the town of Astorga. We strode along with her, assisted by the fact that we'd got talking to her at the 925m summit and it was all downhill to Astorga. We were almost too breathless to speak, but we made it in time for Mass. When I explain to people that the Camino is a place of miracles, I often use Agnieszka as an example. By the end of that day's walking the straps on my rucksack (which had served me well from the start of the first stage) were coming loose and it would be well-nigh impossible to carry it with no straps, especially in view of some of the steep ascents that lay ahead. It turned out that Agnieszka was a horse vet and that she had brought with her the needles and high-strength thread that she uses to stitch up the horses. At the *albergue* that evening she gladly stitched up the straps of my rucksack and they're still intact years later. As the title of my second book suggests, the universe provides!

While Agnieszka was busy sewing up my straps, I was in the kitchen of the *albergue* doing the cooking. We invited a Dutch woman Gerda to join us and we had a feast. We'd caught up with Gerda on the way into the tiny village of El Ganso and she had a most poignant reason for walking the Camino. It had been the dream of her and her husband to walk the Camino together but a few months before their departure he had died. We found out a few days later that everywhere that Gerda stayed along the route she paid for two beds, one for her and one, kept empty, for him.

Agnieszka's reason for walking was also part of a healing process, albeit following a broken relationship. She had split up from her husband and wished the Camino to be part of her coming to terms with that. In the mountains there is a tall, iron cross, Cruz de Ferro, where pilgrims leave a stone to symbolise their journey. This practice may have its origins in the legend which tells that when the cathedral in Santiago was being built, pilgrims were asked to bring a stone for it. I was with Agnieszka the day we reached that cross. She had me wait at the bottom of the huge pile of stones with her camera to take a photo as she went to the top to place her stone and thereby, she hoped, leave behind the painful events of recent years. Some of the stones, including that of Agnieszka, are brought with pilgrims from home. Many of them, some as big as small rocks, have messages written. Some of those messages indicated, as in Gerda's case, that the pilgrimage was being walked in memory of a loved one. It was a most touching place and it indicated both the internationality of the Camino and the multiplicity of reasons that pilgrims set out on their journey.

Yim Soon and I left El Ganso in the dark and in the rain and after a 30 km walk arrived in the picturesque village of El Acebo. There was a wonderful *'donativo' albergue* on the main, narrow, winding, cobbled street and we were warmly welcomed by Javier, the hospitalero. After the communal meal, Javier led us over to the old church for evening prayer and a blessing. As always, it was a special way to end the day. The next day, to the small town of Pieros, was another 30 km trek but it was worth going the extra miles to claim our beds in an interesting sounding 'vegetarian *albergue* with an alternative vibe.' It was also the day to encounter a modern-day Knights Templar.

In the Middle Ages, pilgrims to places like Canterbury might be attacked on the way by bandits and robbers, who would relieve them of money and any precious objects they may have been taking to leave at the Cathedral. So too on the Camino to Santiago, pilgrims could be seen as easy game to the unscrupulous and the Knights Templars were provided to give security en route. This powerful Catholic military monastic organisation was founded in about 1119 and had its headquarters on the Temple Mount in Jerusalem. It was an elite fighting force at the heart of the crusades and at its height it numbered up to 20,000 members. Several Knights Templar strongholds were established along the Camino, including the imposing castle at Ponferrada whose ramparts we walked around that day.

There is a scene in *The Way* where Martin Sheen and his Camino companions find themselves in a sort of hostel run by a man who turns out to be totally crazy. They decide not to stay for the night, fearing he will kill them in their sleep! I was told somewhere along the route that this crazy character is based on a real person who lives at the side of the Camino on the path from Ponferrada. I was very keen to pay a visit!

Sure enough, a few kilometres out of the town we came to a collection of ramshackle and run-down huts, and hanging rather lopsidedly on a pole was the sign 'Knights Templars.' At the entrance perched on a stool was a youngish man who looked like he was high on drugs. He was playing blues songs on a guitar which had just four strings and he seemed to be making up lyrics as he went. He invited us to come in and meet the Knight! Yim Soon was too afraid to go in so I entered with an intrepid young woman who'd been walking with us that day. There was a second young Spanish man and they announced that they were called Hank and Johnny, also that they were the servants of the Knight. They had a large thermos of (lukewarm) coffee which they offered to us and then we were led further into the labyrinth of huts to meet the main man. There was a roaring fire, next to which was sat an old man with an enormous beard. He didn't quite fit my childhood picture of a brave, crusading knight but there you go! There was also a pot of something boiling on the stove and I hoped that it wasn't body parts from murdered pilgrims! It wasn't: it was just vegetable soup, and we took a bowl for the sake of politeness at the chaotic kitchen table before saying that we had to get back on the path. I was rather relieved to be outside again and I said to Hank that I'd do a song before leaving. I sang 'El Camino' and he seemed especially impressed that the chorus was in Spanish and he began to dance

When we arrived later at our vegetarian *albergue* in Pieros I was greeted by a young Belgian woman, Claire who I'd spoken to briefly on the way out of Ponferrada who said she had enjoyed hearing me singing to Hank! She, like Yim Soon, had not dared to enter the modern-day HQ of the Camino Knights Templars! There was a huge communal meal, with not just one but several delicious vegetarian courses plus wine. It was shared with the most fascinating bunch of characters, who were intrigued by the story of my visit to the Knights Templars. Shay, a mime artist from Israel, laughed when I mentioned Hank and Johnny. She had also met them briefly, although to her they'd given their real Spanish names!

One of the pilgrims at Pieros had collected on the way a large bag of chestnuts and so the meal was followed by a communal chestnut eating session. I carried on speaking with Shay till the early hours and then, as there were just three of us in our room (and no snorers!) had my first proper night's sleep on the Camino.

Even with a good night's sleep under my belt Day Five was tough, especially in the morning. The route followed a road for much of the way, even going at times under a motorway, and there seemed to be no other pilgrims around. 'Had they all caught the bus to the next place?' I wondered. Yim Soon and I fell out over something silly and we walked apart for a while, each dwelling in their own misery. Somehow we found reconciliation in the afternoon, and on the final, steep climb to the remote mountain hamlet of La Faba we had a most pleasant conversation with a young Swedish man called Linus. Our *albergue* for the night was a converted outhouse containing eight bunk beds and one of the best showers I will ever have. There was also the chance to have a proper cup of tea with milk. As I sipped my tea whilst waiting for the three-course meal that awaited us, I took a few moments to take stock on our journey to date. We'd had four fantastic days, and there had been one that had been more challenging and where the mood was more subdued. It wasn't a bad return, I reflected. All in all, it was great to be back on the Camino, it was really special to be there with Yim Soon, and as usual there had been some touching encounters with a range of characters.

We had been going at quite a steady pace: thirty to thirty-five kilometres a day for those first five days. It proved to be a bit too much for Yim Soon. We found ourselves in that secluded hamlet in the mountains and Yim Soon's whole body had seized up. And we still had well over 200 km to Santiago. But as said already, the universe provides. On this occasion the universe provided in the form of a masseur known to the woman who ran the small hostel and restaurant where we were staying. She called him and he drove over and gave Yim Soon a rigorous massage and that is one of the best forty euros we will ever spend. She was able to walk again the next day and Santiago was in our sights once more.

By the end of the next day we had passed into the region of Galicia and were in Triacastela, named after the three castles that had once stood there. In the summer this small town of one thousand people sees its population double due to the influx of pilgrims. Yim Soon and I were at about our mid-point to Santiago and had decided to have a break from the 'real' Camino experience in the communal *albergue*s and treat ourselves. For the ridiculous price of about €30 we had a large en-suite room in a tastefully restored former farm building, and right in the middle of the town besides. I revelled in the sight of wooden beams and partially-revealed stone walls as we indulged in the luxury of being able to empty out our rucksacks and rearrange our belongings in neat piles.

It had been a wonderful day from start to finish. My alarm in the *albergue* at La Faba had gone off by mistake at 6.30 a.m. so we'd got up and had left the hamlet in the pitch black and walked by torchlight up the mountain track. It was 5 km to the summit. The stars were coming in and out of vision and when we got a bit higher up we could look down on a blanket of mist floating above the valley. It was utterly magical. The hamlet of O'Cebreiro is at the top, at an altitude of 1,330 m, and it has been a place of welcome for pilgrims for over a thousand years. The large *albergue* had been a collection of abandoned buildings until the Camino regained its popularity towards the end of the twentieth century. Several pilgrims were coming out for a photo session with the sunrise and there were lots of nice encounters with people both then and throughout the day. There was a Californian couple carrying their thirteen-month-old daughter Lucia; there was Kirsten, a German woman who'd stayed with us at La Faba; there was Belén from Madrid, and a little later on her partner Álvero. When we'd first spotted them they'd been walking twenty metres apart! They'd had a falling out that day! "These things happen," I explained to Belén, "yesterday it was us!" In the end the four of us walked together into Triacastela and had a beer.

For much of the day we had been at a fairly high altitude, able to enjoy the wide, open views in each direction. It was such a contrast, in every way, to the previous day when we'd been down at the bottom of the valley and by the motorway and down also in mood. The walk to Triacastela was like heaven in comparison. There was an easy, gradual descent to the town, where we spent a relaxed and convivial evening. After the beer with Belén and Álvaro (who by now had reconciled with one another) we had a cup of tea with a Belgian woman called Leen who explained that her job with the United Nations took her into war-zones and that walking the Camino was a means of healing from post-traumatic stress syndrome. The Camino seemed to be working, from what I could see!

The hotel where we had our luxurious double room had as well a kitchen. I gladly cooked and we invited to join us a young man from Bristol, Patrick and a young German woman, Melissa who said that she was eating only muesli bars each day so as to save money. She also had blisters and looked thoroughly miserable. It was good to be able to give a little bit of kindness and to share hospitality. I had received so many blessings throughout my Camino experience and I was happy to be able to offer something back. Later in the evening, while strolling through the town, we had a first meeting with Patricia from Mexico. It was a peaceful night away from the throng and we were ready for the walk to Sarria. Leaving Triacastela in the morning, the path took us steeply up through woods and it reminded me of the Peak District in England. At the top of the hill there were more spectacular views, more lovely encounters, more photos…

When we reached Sarria there was a sudden upsurge in the number of pilgrims. To qualify for the *Compostela* certificate in Santiago it is necessary to have walked at least 100 km and Sarria is just over 100 km from Santiago so that is where a lot of people begin! In the kitchen of the municipal hostel whilst cooking our pasta we met a lovely young Spanish woman, Pepi, who was teaching at a school in Birmingham and taking advantage of the half-term. I also, when out wandering in the town, saw a man I recognised. It was Martin who is the manager of Waterstones bookshop in Canterbury. You just never know who you're going to bump into on the Camino! Just as that elderly Spanish man had remarked to me two years before, the world is indeed a handkerchief.

The *albergue* in Sarria where we stayed was in a set of grand buildings perched on a hillside and named 'El monasterio de Santa Magdalena.' It had a bit of a converted seminary feel to it, like the place where I'd stayed the year before in Burgos. It was spacious and clean and there weren't too many people there. Few of the bunkbeds in the vast dormitory were taken and, mercifully, there were no snorers (unless the snorer was me!). It was a peaceful and quiet night.

We took advantage again of the large and well-equipped kitchen to make breakfast, which we shared with a few others. Pepi was there, so too Ali and Mike, a couple from Pennsylvania who were walking the Camino for their honeymoon. There was a first meeting with Inga and Carmel, who we would see again at Santiago. It was an almost perfect day. We passed through more beautiful countryside, which had changed quite dramatically across the North of Spain. From the rugged mountains of the Basque country we had then gone through the flat, treeless planes of the *meseta*, and now we were in the verdant mountains of Galicia.

The walk from Sarria to the mid-sized town of Portomarin took us though a rolling, wooded landscape and the sun was shining for us. It was also relatively short at 22 km! We had broken the back of the walking with those first few 30 km-plus days, and the last days would be a little easier; or should I say a little less difficult! We had our first encounter with a lovely Spanish man Ignacio. We saw a lot of him in those final days to Santiago and we would often share beer and fried octopus at the end of a walk. When I asked Ignacio about his reasons for walking the Camino he explained that as a child his family had sometimes gone on holiday to Santiago. He had witnessed group after group of pilgrims arriving in the cathedral square and falling to their knees and bursting into tears and he had decided that one day he needed to find out for himself what it was all about.

We found a €6 *albergue* in Portomarin and it looked as if we could be in for a lively night. There were suddenly lots of Spanish pilgrims, who had started in Sarria, and a large group of them were in that same *albergue* and seemed in the mood to party. What to do! We had opted for the 'real' Camino experience! Ignacio, by contrast, had booked into hotel rooms each night. However, he told us how hard it was to return to his solitary room at the end of the day and how he wished he'd chosen the communal *albergue*s. The grass is always greener...

In the end I had a pleasant enough night in that thirty-bed *albergue*, even if all of those beds were in one dormitory and three of them were occupied by snorers! Plus, by that time on the Camino, with some people having been on the road for weeks or even months, the smell of body odour was now pretty strong! When I accepted that I wouldn't be getting any sleep I got dressed and went downstairs and read a book and relished that time of being alone. I managed a few hours of shut-eye and then we were up with the throng at 6.45 a.m. and on the road in the dark at 7.30. We crossed the spectacular, long bridge out of the town and followed the path up through the woods on the opposite side of the river in the pitch dark. My torch no longer worked but luckily there was a Croatian guy who had also started early and who had a headlamp. The universe provided…again!

Further into the woods Yim Soon met a man from Korea that we'd encountered the previous day and chatted with him. I suddenly found myself on my own in the dark. I sang Psalm 63, which I know by heart, having sung it as part of my morning prayer for many years. I felt an overwhelming sense of 'at oneness' with nature and with the whole of creation as the first light of dawn began to break through. I was also overcome with tears and emotion. I gave thanks for this incredible journey that had begun for me two and a half years before. It was a journey which had traversed my leaving of L'Arche, an organisation I'd been part of for twenty-eight years, and my starting work at another charity, the Irish Chaplaincy. It was a journey that was now nearing its end; its physical end, at any rate.

There was a discernible spring in my step throughout that day. Yim Soon, the Korean guy and me stopped for breakfast at a roadside café after 8 km: two fried eggs, bacon, bread and *café con leche*. I had earned it! And then with stomach (as well as heart) full, it was back on the road. I chatted in French with a group of teenagers from Brittany. We bumped into people who now seemed like old friends: Patricia, Agnieszka, Ignacio; plus Joe from Slovenia and Larry the drummer.

We made it into Palas de Rei, 25 km from Portomarin and it was our turn to buy the beer and the octopus! There's a great photo of a group of very happy-looking pilgrims sitting under an umbrella outside a bar: Yim Soon and me, Ignacio, Patricia, and a woman called Sonia who we had picked up somewhere along the way! Thanks to our early start there was time for a sleep and a shower, two cups of tea with milk (luxury!) and a relaxed stroll around the supermarket to get the ingredients for cooking in our pleasant *albergue* called 'Buen Camino.' As usual Yim Soon and I invited whoever was around to eat with us. It was wonderful for us to be able to share in this way with our fellow pilgrims.

The following night in the small and attractive town of Arzúa we stayed at 'O Santa' which was probably the nicest place we'd been in after the hotel at Triacastela. Although it was a communal *albergue*, we each had a spacious bed in its own compartment and with its own light. That was palatial compared to some of the places where we'd stayed! There was also a well-equipped kitchen where Yim Soon and I cooked spaghetti and sauce for ourselves and Patricia. She was most appreciative, so too of the bottle of red wine from the region which we opened. The host was a friendly woman called Monica who gave us some local cheese as a gift. On arrival into Arzúa, the final major centre of population before Santiago, Ignacio had bought the beer and octopus and we'd also had time to attend the pilgrim Mass in the old church in the town square.

It had been a great day, one of the highlights of which had been meeting Johnny English! At the side of the road in a tiny village there was a garden with a sign hanging from a tree that said 'Welcome to the house of Johnny English.' There was table in the garden laden with little treats and inviting a donation. From the house there appeared a man whose accent straight away betrayed his origins in the West Midlands of England. David was excited to hear that I'd grown up in Coventry and made us tea and told us his story. He had walked the Camino and the experience had touched him so much that he had had tattooed down the length of his torso the route and all the main stops from Saint-Jean-Pied-de-Port to Santiago. And he lifted his T-shirt to show us! Then he had bought an old house in a village on the Camino route and was in the process of converted an outbuilding into accommodation for pilgrims. He told of how he'd been going to bed one night when his neighbour, an elderly man who spoke little English, had called out, "Goodnight Johnny Eengleesh!"

I was awake early in the morning for a wander in the town and a cup of tea on the balcony of the *albergue* which overlooked the main street of Arzúa. We used the kitchen again to make breakfast before setting off for our second last day of walking. At a café stop on the way we met Pepi as well as lots of other Camino friends, old and new. It was hard to believe that the journey was almost over.

That Camino journey, which had begun for me over two years previously, came to an unexpected but blessed moment of completion on the evening before walking the final twelve of the 500 miles from St-Jean-Pied-de-Port on the French side of the Pyrenees. A group of us were sitting around a table in a pilgrim hostel in Pedrouzo eating, drinking, chatting and laughing. There were three Brazilians, including Ariel who we'd met on that first day out of León. There was Nancy and Tim, the New Yorkers that we'd also met on that first morning. Then there was Yim Soon, Ignacio and me. A Canadian man called Claude appeared and sat with us. He was doing the Camino by bike so didn't know any of us who were walking but he said that he been in the dormitory upstairs and had heard the chatter and the laughter and that something had drawn him towards us.

We were sharing Camino stories and then Claude suggested that we each tell of a particular highlight of our Camino journey. Ignacio, who had been so generous with buying the post-walk beers and octopus, confided that he had been made redundant some months previously. It was the first I knew of that. He went on to say that the Camino had taught him to see what was truly important in life, like spending time with family and friends. Nancy told us about the generosity of a young German woman. She had gone with Nancy and translated for her at the hospital when a foot injury had threatened to end her pilgrimage on the very first day. Then she'd given Nancy a pair of sandals which fitted perfectly and in which she was able to walk until she could wear her boots again. One of the young Brazilians, Mathieu, was in tears as he spoke of the death of his mother four months before and his regret at being away at the time. He went on to say that on the Camino his mother had appeared to him in a dream and had said goodbye to him. Ariel told us amidst a mixture of tears and laughter how after the Camino he was going to be a better person: "To my girlfriend, to my parents, to my cat and my dog, even to my table."

When it came to my turn, I explained that I was on the Camino to celebrate and to give thanks: for all that had happened in my life since I began my first stage in April 2015; for our children; and for twenty-five years of marriage. And I said that a highlight was doing this third and final stage with Yim Soon. There was loud applause and cheering in the group, and yet another toast. We had each lived something profound on the Camino and it was a blessing that we had the opportunity to share together on this last evening before Santiago something of the essence of that. I bumped into Claude again in Santiago and told him that he had been the channel of some kind of sacred energy for the group. He explained again, "I was just drawn to something and I had to come."

We had one more important task to perform at Pedrouzo. It was October 26th and our daughter Miran's twenty-first birthday. We made a large sign saying 'Happy 21st Miran' and had a photo taken of us holding it up which was then sent to our beloved daughter.

Before going to bed we arranged to meet Nancy and Tim, who were staying elsewhere, at 6.30 a.m. so we could do that final walk together. Our rendezvous didn't work out and we ended up walking the hour or two in the dark with a young Croatian couple. We made steady progress through the eucalyptus woods, guided by the light of the stars, and at a certain point we found ourselves going along the perimeter fence of Santiago airport. We were on the outskirts of the city as dawn began to break. I was finding it tough going due to an empty stomach but we eventually found a food kiosk next to the statue at Gozo, which is the first place from which can be seen the cathedral 6.5 km away. As I munched my bacon roll and sipped my *café con leche* we spotted Belén and Álvaro and chatted for a while with them.

I had the wind in my sails again as we got closer to the centre of the city and as we passed familiar faces: Patricia, Larry the drummer; another Spanish couple, Vicennes and Loli, who were having a coffee before the final stretch. When we eventually reached the Cathedral gate we decided, perhaps unwisely, not to go straight to the Cathedral, rather to try to find accommodation and somewhere to leave our bags. The former monastery where I'd hoped to stay was *completo*, full, and in the end we had to leave our rucksacks in a €5 drop place before we could enter the Cathedral. I had got quite stressed in the fruitless search for accommodation and the entry into the Cathedral plaza was altogether an anti-climax and a disappointment. I was also a bit put off by how busy and touristy the city was. To cap it all, the Cathedral was covered in scaffolding at the time for renovation work! It was a far cry from the falling to knees and sobbing that Ignacio had witnessed of arriving pilgrims when on his childhood holidays!

We made it into the Cathedral just in time for the noonday Pilgrims' Mass. We even had the swinging of the *botafumeiro*, the enormous incense burner that requires seven people to lift and swing from one side of the cathedral to the other. It was good to be there; it just wasn't the amazing spiritual experience I'd expected it to be. I'd been looking forward to that moment for years, ever since I'd seen Martin Sheen in *The Way* and his arrival into the Cathedral and the swinging of the *botafumeiro* and the tears running down his cheeks. 'One day,' I'd thought, 'I want to see that.' Like everything about my arrival into Santiago it was a little bit of a let-down.

Our priority after Mass was finding accommodation in the busy city, as well as getting something to eat. My hunger wasn't doing anything to help my mood. We were led by Patricia to the little hotel where she was staying and although it was *completo*, the woman running it kindly called her friend up the road and we were welcomed a few minutes later at the 'Hospedaje Mera.' The lovely woman running that place was excited to hear that we were celebrating our twenty-fifth wedding anniversary and gave us a room for two nights with a balcony that overlooked one of the main thoroughfares to the Cathedral. And for just €35 a night!

We returned to the Cathedral square at 6 p.m., where a large group of pilgrims was assembling, as arranged earlier. A lot of them had started together back at St-Jean-Pied-de-Port and they were being marshalled by Inga and Carmel to go for a meal. I was still feeling a bit out of sorts, and didn't want to be part of such a big gathering. For the previous ten days our life had been centred around walking, from one place to the next. Our job each day was to pack the rucksack in the morning, and then put one step after the next following those yellow arrows. What was my purpose in life now that I wasn't walking, now that we'd reached the destination? Who was I? Was I still a pilgrim? Or just a tourist now? I needed to be on my own just at that moment and went into the Cathedral for ten quiet minutes. When I came out again there was just Yim Soon and Ignacio left from the group. We did what we had done every day at that time. We found a bar and we had beer and octopus and we told our Camino stories and shared how we felt. We recalled that blessed time we'd had in the *albergue* at Pedrouzo the night before. It was just what I needed.

Ignacio went to the pilgrim Mass at 7.30, while Yim Soon and I wandered in the streets of the old town. We returned to the Cathedral an hour later and were delighted to meet some of those wonderful people we'd shared our lives with in the previous days and to have a big photo-shoot. Besides Ignacio, there was Pepi, plus the Brazilians, Ariel, Miguel and Mathieu. There was also Inga and Carmel.

Now I was ready to enjoy the night-life of Santiago, and we all headed to the very lively Rua do Franco. Pilgrim? Tourist? Whatever! We sat out on the pavement terrace of a restaurant, having gathered together some of those beloved people who had touched our hearts, and some new ones too. We drank beer, we ate hamburgers. And how we roared with laughter, as we told some of the stories from those incredible few weeks. Who had produced the biggest blisters? Who had been in a dormitory with the loudest snorer? Who had met the modern-day, real-life Knights Templar on the way? What on earth would we do with ourselves now that we weren't walking? How would we keep alive the spirit of the Camino?

The icing on the cake came just before we were about to leave. There appeared Shay and Claire and a couple of the others that we'd spent such an enjoyable evening with at the vegetarian *albergue* in Pieros. As was often the case on the Camino, it was like seeing long-lost friends again. A bit later in the evening I got a message from Shay to say they'd found a guitar in the place where they were saying and would I like to come and sing for them. It was tempting but their place was a bit out of the city. Anyway, we needed to say our goodbyes to those who would be leaving in the morning. There followed multiple embraces and the exchanging of numbers. And finally we said a sad farewell to our dear friend Ignacio. We wandered slowly back to Hospedaje Mera and we slept well.

I was up early the next day and happily wandered through the city in the dark. I spotted a young German man who was setting off for Finisterre (more of that later). It was great to be out at that hour and to be alive and to have had that Camino experience, and to have shared the final part of it with Yim Soon. Back at the hotel as I waited for her to get up I sat contentedly on the balcony as the city slowly awoke to another day. We had coffee and croissant in a little café and did what I'd enjoyed doing so many times on the Camino, sitting for a while and watching the world go by. Then we meandered a bit in those ancient streets before taking our place at 11.30 a.m in the cathedral. We spotted one after another familiar face as they arrived for the noonday pilgrim Mass. It was all very moving. And then as the service neared its end I spied seven men in monastic garb over by an enormous pillar. They were untying the ropes that hold the *botafumeiro* in place. And then it started to swing, a little at first and then eventually from one side of the cathedral to the other.

The *botafumeiro* has its origins in the Middle Ages, when the pilgrims would be so smelly after their long journey that the air would need to be purified! It truly was a purification for me, and finally the tears came. They were streaming down my face, and they were tears of pure joy. I looked over at the twenty or thirty priests who were concelebrating the Mass. There was a friendly Korean Jesuit who we had spoken to on one of the final walks. He, like several of the priests, was filming that incredible spectacle on his phone. It was a nice detail. I looked back at the congregation and spotted Claude and a few others of the amazing people we had journeyed with. I felt such a deep sense of gratitude. As I explained to those whose English was good enough to get the pun, it was the cherry on the icing on the Camino cake!

Yim Soon and I had lunch at the café of the kind woman who Patricia had directed us to the day before and who had called her friend at the Hospedaje Mera. She cooked for us herself and we chatted a bit with her as we ate. We wandered the streets again in the afternoon and carried on bumping into pilgrims. We met Ali and Mike the honeymoon couple and arranged to see them for a meal in the evening. There was Mick from Ireland who had been telling hilarious stories the night before. And then who should we see next to a fountain but Claude and his bike. I told him once more how he had been the channel of some kind of sacred energy on that last evening before Santiago, in the *albergue* at Pedrouzo. He replied again that he'd been drawn by something and he just had to come. We blessed one another one final time and embraced and he disappeared down the lane on his bike.

We were back at the cathedral for the 7.30 p.m. pilgrims' Mass and witnessed yet another swinging of the *botafumeiro*. Apparently it requires a wealthy pilgrim to pay a fee of about €400 in order to compensate the seven swingers, who aren't monks at all, rather local guys making a bit of extra cash! Business is business, and always has been in places of pilgrimage! Again we were right at the front of the cathedral, as had been recommended by someone on the way to Santiago, and so once more had ringside seats for this unforgettable sight. It's possible for pilgrims to walk for weeks or months and then not see the *botafumeiro* at all when they get to Santiago. We ended up seeing it three times.

We met up with Ali and Mike as arranged and had an enjoyable meal with them: they at the start of their married journey, we twenty-five years into ours. It was a pleasure to be able to treat them and they were most appreciative. We strolled back to the Hospedaje Mera through those sacred streets one final time. Our Camino was well and truly complete.

We flew home from Santiago early next day. Some, like the German guy I'd seen in the morning, keep on walking for three days to Finisterre which is on the coast. In ancient times this was believed to be the end of the world: hence the name, which literally means the finish of the earth. My friend James had gone all the way to Finisterre in 2015.

Another person who kept on walking is Craig Smith, who is Head of Chaplaincy at Chelmsford prison.

Craig is a pagan and explained to me the Roman pagan belief that the path from Santiago to Finisterre was a place where souls ascended to heaven. For him, then, this part of the walk was the true completion of the Camino.

Craig set out on his first Camino in 2019. After a year of prison chaplaincy he was approaching burnout, and with the lease ending on his flat and the opportunity to take eight weeks off work he decided to do a long-distance walk. He'd heard of the Camino, so on Good Friday he ordered the John Brierley book on Amazon and then on May 1st he flew to Biarritz. He hadn't planned how he was going to get to St-Jean-Pied-de-Port but met a few guys who took him into their taxi, then had lunch with him in St Jean.

He booked into an *albergue* in the town and told me that he spent the next six weeks simply getting up in the morning and walking. It was for him "a wonderful, life-changing experience."

…PILGRIMS' TALES…

Journey to the end of the Earth

I got into a set routine over those six weeks: get up at 6 a.m., pack bag, have a hot chocolate, walk, find a bed for the night, have a beer, eat dinner. You don't have to think about what you're doing; you don't have to think where you're going: you just follow those yellow arrows. You have those eight hours a day, and you can use the time for chit-chat or you can use that space to think. I did a lot of thinking in that time. I thought about my life and all that had happened to me. It was like the Twelve Step programme of AA. In the first steps there is a contemplation of the things that have been done in one's life. Then there is a reflection on the decisions that were made and how they affected other people, and who one needs now to say sorry to.

My Camino was split into three stages. The first third was physical, the second third mental, and the final third spiritual. I had the time and space to put to bed all of my personal demons and then to have the most wonderful spiritual experience walking across the North of Spain. The conversations I had with people on the way helped me to think on a deep level about what I believed, and that in itself was for me a profound spiritual experience.

I had done other long-distance walks prior to the Camino. I had done the eighty-seven-mile Ridgeway Walk from Avebury in Wiltshire to Ivinghoe Beacon in Buckinghamshire. The difference for me between that and a pilgrimage route is 'intent.' On a pilgrimage route there is also the business of walking from A to B but you are side by side with people who are doing it for an intentionally spiritual reason. You kind of get sucked into it in a great and glorious way. And you can't be surrounded by that and not be profoundly affected. Even the most atheistic of atheists end up saying things like 'The way will provide!'

When you're in that liminal space you can't help but see it as a serendipitous and spiritual experience; like being given a blister plaster by a fellow pilgrim just when I needed it. Another time I came across a Korean woman in her 50s who was sitting on a bench in floods of tears. I went up to her and touched her on the arm and asked if she was O.K. She said through her tears, "It's just all so beautiful."

The Camino was life-changing for me. It was also physically tough and I hadn't been prepared at all for that first day's walk up the mountain and over the Pyrenees. Three-quarters of the way up, my legs were like jelly and I feared I wouldn't even complete the first day. Just at that moment a guy appeared at my side. I never saw him again after that day and I don't even know his name but he comforted me and got me to the top of the mountain and down the other side and into Roncesvalles. On the second day's walk I knew I would need a proper walking stick and said to myself, 'If there is a God, let me find a walking stick.' There at the side of the road was the perfect stick which seemed to be calling out, 'Craig, please take me!' I did indeed take it, and with much gratitude, and it served me well all the way to Santiago, and beyond.

One of those I met on the way was a woman who said that the Camino had helped to restore her faith in human nature. She worked in a high-stress office in the City of London and explained that people did things for her because it was their job and they wanted something from her. On the Camino, by contrast, she had the experience of people helping her because they wanted to help her.

There are lasting benefits for me of having done the Camino. I'm truly at peace with myself now, and I've learnt to listen to myself. I recognise that I need to take that time every year to 're-set.' In a curious way, I came to understand a bit better how it is for those in prison. On the Camino, you sort of lose track of which day it is as you slip into that steady, daily routine. It shed new light for me on the routine in prison where one day is much like any other for those incarcerated.

Craig, England

Craig remembers as well with a smile that when he reached Finisterre for that first time in 2019 he said, 'Never again!' When I asked him why, he said simply, 'The pain; it hurts; I was battered by the end of it!' His feet were in shreds, having walked in trainers; and he had carried too much stuff in his rucksack. However, as he and I and countless others have found as well, the Camino is kind of addictive. Craig would be back for more; and so would I…

CHAPTER 3

SANTIAGO (III)

On May 1st 2023, four years to the day after Craig Smith had flown to Biarritz to begin his first Camino journey, Yim Soon and I were on a plane to Porto to do the Portuguese Coastal Camino. Craig had already done that, besides a second stint on the Camino Francés. He had started the Portuguese leg in Lisbon and told me ruefully how the interminably long cobbled section to Porto was a killer on the feet!

It was my first time in Porto. The group of eight on the BBC *Pilgrimage* mini-series of 2023 had passed through this stunning city which rises steeply on either side of the Douro River. They had been following a pilgrimage route south to the Catholic shrine of Fatima. On our way Yim Soon and I would pass a handful of pilgrims who were doing likewise. Also heading south were the two men we met at the Cathedral as we were all getting our Camino passports. Born in Bavaria, Peter and Karl had both lived for decades in the States. Peter told me how much he preferred British to American humour and that he had been a particular fan of the 70s sitcom *Are you being served!* The encounters, sometimes a little surreal, with interesting characters had already begun and we hadn't even begun to walk.

We left the Cathedral in the direction of the famous Dom Luís bridge which straddles the two sides of the city but followed instead the sound of a busker in a cavernous, walled area. It was a guitarist, Benjamin, who is a German living in Dublin and whose previous pitch had been on Grafton Street. I ended up doing a few songs, including Yim Soon's favourite *When you were sweet 16*, and my own song about a bar in Belfast *Fibber McGees*, then Yim Soon and I did our Korean party-piece, the 80s hit *Sarangun onjeana kujariea*, Love is always in that place. A young woman watching said it had brought tears to her eyes.

The music continued through the evening. We passed a large group of black-cloaked young women singing Portuguese traditional songs and dancing. Later, while watching the sunset from a crowded hillock next to the bridge, a local busker was doing a great *Coldplay* set. And when we wandered back over the bridge to Ribeira Square to eat, there was yet more good live street music from Dutch Jenny and her accompanist on guitar. And we spotted Benjamin again, on the hunt for another pitch. It had been a special first day, and we hadn't even started on the Camino.

The first day of actual walking was one of highs and lows. Such is the Camino; and such is life. It had begun on an extreme high. I woke as dawn was breaking and returned to the Dom Luís bridge to see the sunrise over the hills and the valley. There was just me plus four Korean men who were also out sunrise-spotting at that early hour. We had to step aside for a few moments to let a tram go by. I was struck by how nearly everyone on the tram was glued to their phones and completely missing what was one of the most incredible sunrises I'd ever seen! I told that story several times in the coming days, adding that I was often the person missing what was right in front of my nose.

After a cup of coffee in our room (which had also supplied us on arrival with two very welcome mini-bottles of Port!) we went to an art deco McDonalds for breakfast, then took the metro to Matosinhos in order to miss out the 11 km hike through the suburbs of the city. We walked up onto the long bridge crossing the river and we were on our way, following those yellow arrows and conch shells. We got into conversation immediately with a group of Californians who were also setting off. I chatted with Bill who had just returned from walking for twelve days in Italy from Lucca to Rome. He had walked the Camino Francés before and explained his motivation as being simply that he liked walking! He went on to say that he was an atheist and he was adamant that for him it was not a spiritual experience, although he could recognise that for many people the act of walking on an ancient pilgrimage route would be significant.

A little later we met two more guys from the States and I chatted with Kurt as Yim Soon walked a bit further back with Pat. Kurt told me a tale from his time the year before on the Camino Francés. He had reached the age of sixty-three wondering whether he needed to slow down. As part of that process he decided to take a few months out and walk the Camino, having watched *The Way*. He had developed an acute pain in his body which appeared to ease when he slowed down! But still he couldn't resist the urge to go faster! He told me of a pleasant encounter with a Belgian woman and about their lack of a common language. She spoke Flemish, French and German, while he spoke English and Spanish, so whenever they passed one another on the way they would simply wave and call out *bonjour*. One day he was at the top of a mountain and praying, "God, if you want me to slow down in my life please give me a sign." Just at that moment, the Belgian woman appeared as if from nowhere and looked him in the eyes and said in perfect English, "You really need to slow down!" I mentioned to Kurt that I'd once given a reflection on a retreat in which I'd made the observation that throughout the Bible interesting things happen on mountains!

It was tough going in the early afternoon as the temperature rose into the high 20s and with no shade. I was hot and bothered and my rucksack was digging into my back and shoulders. "Why are we doing this?" I was asking myself. We were going along a very touristy stretch of sea-front and it just didn't feel like I was on a pilgrimage or having any kind of spiritual experience. I felt a bit disappointed and I wasn't able to fully appreciate the incredible beauty of the surroundings.

To make matters worse, I ignored Yim Soon's advice to check my phone to see where we were staying. We ended up overshooting by fifteen minutes, which meant an added half an hour onto an already interminably long walk. We were both in bad moods when we finally arrived at Casa Sonia, which was a couple of miles *before* the town of Vila do Conde which I'd been heading for. Our moods got even worse when we were asked to pay, with me being convinced I'd paid in advance. We remonstrated with the woman on reception, who turned out be the eponymous Sonia, but to no avail. I was really fed up, and we were wondering if this was going to happen at every place along the way! How easy it is to suspect that the world is conspiring against us! We had a large and tastefully decorated room with a long balcony and sea view, and I couldn't appreciate it at all. And then the phone rang. Sonia had contacted Booking.com and there was a friendly woman called Rita in Barcelona who looked at all of our bookings and it transpired that it had been my mistake. I promptly went down and apologised to Sonia. In the meantime we had gone down to the beach and I had gone into the sea and immersed myself in the big waves and it had been the start of the healing of the hurts and disappointments of the day.

The gentle healing continued in the evening at *Terrasse*, the Italian restaurant on the seafront. The waiter was friendly, the food and locally produced wine delicious. And finally, there was a little bit of chat with three ladies from Geneva who were curious about us! The day ended well and Yim Soon and I were able to laugh about some of the mishaps that had befallen us along the way.

After the trials and tribulations of Day 1, we were richly rewarded on Day 2. I woke again to the sound of the dawn chorus and we were on the road at 6.45 a.m. We just kept on going and didn't stop for breakfast until 9.30 by which time we were halfway to Esposende where we would spend the night. We had spoken on the way to Jörg and Jenny from Germany. For Jenny it was her first Camino and she was taking some time out after finishing a stressful job and before beginning something different. Another German called Jörg (who I subsequently christened Jörg 2) was also taking a break of three weeks to "calm down" as he put it and to be with people who were more peaceful than in his workplace. He was happy to get away from his bosses, of which he said he had five, all of whom acted like kings! He had planned to come on the Camino in 2020 for a week but Covid had put paid to that. His dream had grown over that time to two and then three weeks and he declared to me, "It's now or never!"

The walking and even the rucksack-carrying was so much easier than on the first day and by 2 p.m. we had reached our destination, where we were warmly welcomed by Ana at the Esposende Guest House. I was touched to see that she had with her a copy of Raynor Winn's *The Salt Path*. I told her that I'd just finished reading it the week before and that Jörg 1 had also just read it in German! Ana explained that an English girl had left it the week before. This book was to run like a thread through my Portuguese Camino.

We managed to miss the rain whilst walking and it was soothing to sit in our room and listen to the gentle sound it made. I was really hungry as we hadn't eaten any lunch so we ventured out to a café recommended by Ana and ended up having a glass of (strong!) Belgian beer with Daniel from Atlanta and I also ate a delicious ham and cheese toastie to keep us going until the evening. My ideal walking rhythm, as it had been in the past, was to set off early, as we'd done on that day, stop somewhere for a late breakfast and then crack on to the end without much by way of lunch. The only problem with that, as other pilgrims commented too, was that restaurants in Portugal and Spain don't open for dinner until late in the evening!

Back in our room in the guest house Yim Soon took a nap and I began to feel rather flat as the effects of the Belgian beer wore off. I was also beginning to yearn for a bit of religious ritual. I didn't want this to be 'just' a nice long-distance walk; I wished for there to be some kind of spiritual experience. After all, it was the Camino; wasn't I supposed to be feeling spiritual? I strolled through the narrow streets of the small, attractive town and went into a chapel on the square that was open. I spent a bit of time in prayer but still it didn't really lift my mood. I walked further and came across the main church and that was also open so I went in and prayed some more and that didn't lift my mood either. I made my way back to the estuary next to which the town had grown up and felt the wind envelop me. That's something which usually energises me, but still I was feeling a bit sorry for myself.

I woke Yim Soon and we went out to an Italian restaurant and had a sumptuous meal of pizza and spaghetti carbonara and salad, accompanied by a bottle of local red which was as nice as that of the previous evening. Little by little, the mood of each of us lifted. There was a family on the next table with a young boy and we began to attract his attention. From that we got into conversation with the Portuguese mother, and her mother who was feeding her grandchild, and the Spanish father. It was a wonderful mixture of Portuguese, Spanish and English and the grandmother told us how she drove every year with her friend to Santiago. It was a special moment of connection. We wandered a little in the town afterwards and came to the church and, although it was after 9 p.m. there was a communion service taking place for a surprisingly large congregation. We took our places. I had well and truly had my bit of religious ritual added to the great walking.

Day 3 was an almost perfect day from start to finish and the day that I began to truly feel the spirit of the Camino. I woke as usual at 5.40 a.m. to the sound of the first birdsong and was out strolling in the narrow streets of Esposende as the dawn broke. We were on the road by 7 o'clock and had an hour's walking under our belts by the time we reached Marinhas, where we came to a little supermarket which had an area where breakfast could be bought. There were two pilgrims already in place, sipping their coffee. We enjoyed *café con leche* with croissants, also the sight of the local people coming in and out and greeting one another. Yim Soon and I had a brief moment of tension whilst I tried, unsuccessfully at first, to navigate us to the Camino route. When I was on the Camino Francés I managed to find the way with no phone at all, although I did have my John Brierley. So far on the Camino Portuguese I was stubbornly refusing to use my 'Peregrino Online' phone app too much but clearly I would need to use my data a bit more so as to access the Google Maps.

For the first two days it had simply been a case of keeping the sea on your left. Today's path veered away from the coast and, when we eventually found it, went through first pine trees and then a eucalyptus forest. We also passed a waterfall. It was a most welcome change from walking by the ocean and it was a treat for the eyes, also the nose. Following a heavy downpour there were all kinds of interesting smells in the air.

It was also a great day of encounters. Back in Marinhas I'd chatted a bit with Vicente from Spain who said he liked to walk "slowly, slowly" and look at everything around him. In the village church an elderly man appeared and offered to stamp our pilgrim passports. He also gave us a prayer card of St Joseph. It turned out that he was the priest and he was delighted to perform this little ministry for pilgrims.

From the church, the path climbed gradually uphill out of the village. We caught up with Jörg 1 and Jenny and walked and talked with them for a large part of the day. Jörg began to tell his story. After all, that's what people do on the Camino; that's what people have always done on pilgrimage. There is something about the act of walking that draws out our story. There is also something about us being in an unfamiliar place, out of our comfort zone; perhaps even the fact that we'll probably never see each other again. All of these factors seem to bring a particular openness and honesty. Jörg's story was quite remarkable. Forty years before, following a kind of dizzy spell, he'd been given a diagnosis of MS and the doctor said he'd need to go on medication. Jörg called his then girlfriend and said, "Bring me my running shoes!" Two years later he ran his first marathon, and since then he has walked several Camino routes.

I reminded Jörg that his story resembled that of Raynor Winn's husband Moth in *The Salt Path*. Moth had been given a terminal diagnosis in about 2015 and was taking medication to try to control the symptoms. Having lost their home and everything they had, the couple decided on an impulse to walk the South-West Coastal path in England. At a certain point, Moth ran out of his medication but realised a few days later that his physical condition had actually improved. As long as he kept walking he was fine. Jörg told me something similar. Moth is still going fairly strong, several years after he was told that his rare condition would kill him. And Jörg is still walking Caminos four decades after being given his diagnosis.

We found a welcome café on the road just before mid-day and just before a big downpour. Jörg and Jenny arrived, so too the couple of guys we'd seen at breakfast. One of them was on his fourth stint on the Portuguese Coastal Camino. His day job was running a bar in Holland. He explained to me he meets a lot of "fake" people in the bar, but on the Camino "people tell the truth." He went on to say that, "You might never see the person again; why not tell the truth? No need to be fake." He said he came on the Camino to clear his mind.

Downpour over, we set off again, back up into the woods. I met Austrian-born Barbara who lives in the States. She told me she was Jewish and that Jerusalem was for her a highly spiritual place. "It's where the events in the Bible actually took place," she pointed out to me animatedly. She had been struck too at the sight of people throwing themselves to the ground at the holy places.

On the Camino Francés there are many *donativo* rest and refreshment spots for pilgrims in the middle of woods or other random places. We came across our first such place on the Portuguese route just when I was ready for some lunch. Who was sitting there already but Jörg 2! I duly introduced him to Jörg 1! Leah from Croatia arrived, also Stefan from Frankfurt, plus the two Dutch guys. There was a gregarious local man whose mission in life was to provide snacks and drinks for pilgrims, for which he invited a donation. I chatted with him a bit and then he went off to get more boiled eggs. It was a great place of encounter and, as said, reminiscent of many such places on the Camino Francés.

I spoke next to Stefan, who was one of several people I met who said the Camino had been on their bucket list. He had in fact spent 2016 doing everything on his bucket list. He had a holiday in Italy with his sons, ran his first marathon, and did the Camino Francés! We met in the evening in a restaurant in the town and he told us that for him, pilgrimage was about coming closer to God. He also shared with us how he always brought a question with him. In 2016 the question was whether God existed and the answer, he discovered for himself, was yes. This time the question was what he was to do with the rest of his life now he had taken early retirement at the age of fifty-five. He also said to us that he had realised through the Camino that things like salary level and prestige that he had previously thought of as constituting a successful life were not so. Rather it was how we treated one another.

Our eventual arrival in the old hill-top town of Viano do Castelo after our 28 km hike was across a long, high bridge spanning the river. We had been richly rewarded during the day and a further treat was finding that we had a whole apartment to ourselves. There was even a little terrace which afforded fine views over the rooftops of the old quarter and right up to a church perched on a wooded hillside. As was the case again and again, the Camino took us through stunning countryside but also right into the heart of beautifully preserved medieval towns.

It was 23 km from Viano do Castalo to Moledo on Day 4 and it was yet another great day on the Camino from start to finish. I was out and about at 6 a.m. wandering in the historic centre of the town and along by the seafront, then we were on the road at 7. For a while we followed the alternative 'green' route along by the sea but then decided to return to the official 'yellow' route so as to find somewhere for breakfast. Whilst wandering in some residential streets a car pulled up and a very friendly woman asked in English if we needed any help. When I explained that we were looking for breakfast she had us get into the car and drove to a nearby café. It was closed so she continued down the main road, in the opposite direction to where she was headed. The second café she came to was also closed so she drove further still until we finally came to a café that was open. She chatted about her husband of thirty-one years and her two sons, similar in age to our children and one of whom is called Tiago, as in Santiago! Her name was Marta and I told her she was an angel. She seemed as delighted by the encounter as we were.

We crossed the busy road to the café and met our first Korean on this Camino. Kim told us that he was seventy-one, had started two weeks earlier in Lisbon and was tired! He showed us his custom-made app with his own routes and offered it to me to download. I politely declined. We enjoyed our cheese and ham toasties and *café con leches* and had a first meeting with Ingvild from Norway and French Andrea. And then we were off back to the official yellow trail. Like the day before, it was an undulating dirt path through fir and eucalyptus forest. For me it was more interesting than following the coastline constantly. I enjoyed passing by old houses and farms and seeing the explosion of spring colour in the form of azaleas and rhododendrons and roses and foxgloves. There was even the delicious smell of a jasmine in bloom.

Our second bit of kindness from the locals came when we got talking to two women who were walking along the trail. They told us they were on their way to a hidden waterfall and lagoon and offered to take us. We happily followed them along a narrow track through the woods. They left us at the lagoon and went back further down-river. I seized the moment. I took off my clothes and dived in off the rocks and swam and it felt like a ritual purification. Back on the path later we caught up with Ingvild and found out a bit about her and her children, also similar in age to ours. In the town of Ancora we ate with her our first 'Pilgrims menu.' It was a big, tasty meal accompanied by a cold beer and followed by crème caramel made by the woman who ran the place. All for just over ten euros each.

On the way through the centre of the town a group of people called out to us from the opposite side of the square. I wasn't sure at first who it was then realised it was the five Californians we'd met at the very start. They were having a beer out on a terrace and were looking very pleased with themselves. We went over and exchanged greetings.

We'd almost done our distance for the day when we left the Californians to have their late lunch. Our stopping place for the night was Moledo, a small seaside village a few kilometres before the larger town of Caminhas where most people were heading for, and from where the boat over to Spain would be taken. After checking in to the hostel, Yim Soon and I made the short walk down to the beach and lay there in the glorious sunshine. I spent a bit of time being blissfully battered by the tall, powerful Atlantic waves. It was more purification.

Those waves are ideal for wind surfing we discovered later when speaking to Richard from Miami who was spending a few days enjoying his passion. He told us that the thermal North wind would arrive in a couple of days' time to create the perfect conditions for his sport. Also staying at 'Xicotina' on the main street through the village of Moledo were Christian and Mirjam, a charming couple from Potsdam who had just walked their first day on the Camino. We ate together in the evening on the picnic bench in the garden. We had bought food in the local shop and for the first time on this trip I had enjoyed both shopping, the chatting with the shop-keeper and the cooking. The eating was good as well! So too being with Christian and Mirjam and sharing about our children, our travels, and other things besides. As recommended by the man in the shop earlier we had on the table a bottle of *vino verde* which he proudly pointed out was found nowhere else in the world except the North of Portugal and in a bit of North-Western Spain. Uniquely for a red wine it is at its best when served cold. I had duly put it in the fridge which meant that we did indeed have it at its best.

I asked Mirjam what had prompted her to begin her Camino from Porto the year before. "I read a book in German," she explained, "about an English couple who walk around the South-West coastline." Yet another person I was meeting on the Camino had been inspired by *The Salt Path*, which Jörg had informed me the day before was top of the best-seller list in Germany. I told them Jörg's story, and how it resembled that of Raynor Winn's husband Moth in the book. "That gives me goosebumps," Mirjam declared.

It was good to wake in the morning of Day 5 to the sound of rain and to have a gentle, slow start to that, our short day of walking. It was also the day that we would leave Portugal behind and enter Spain and the region of Galicia. We drank coffee and chatted more with Christian and Mirjam in the cosy lounge of the hostel and I told them that Francisco the owner had explained how he'd renovated it eight years before and that it had previously been a convent and then a casino! Just before saying our farewells, another German woman Kirsty advised us to avoid the main path but to take 'the road less travelled' which was through a forest running alongside the beach. She explained how the forest is sacred to the local people, and it was great advice. Just as Kirsty had said, we came out at the Minho River which divides northern Portugal from Spain and there was a little wooden hut where we could buy our tickets for the taxi speedboat. It was just the two of us plus a woman from the Czech Republic who were passengers for the brief but exciting crossing. The ferryman set us down on the beach on the other side of the estuary and we clambered out on the sand and were now in Spain.

It was a pleasant route, first through the pine trees skirting the bottom of a mountain and then emerging eventually into A Guarda, an attractive fishing town with the houses painted a variety of bright colours. It was there that we saw yet again the five Californians and, as we always did, we cheerfully greeted one another. We'd also spoken more with James and Carmelita from Idaho who we'd said hello to the day before in the restaurant where we'd had lunch. James was carrying an extremely large rucksack and sometimes that of his partner too since she was struggling with her legs. His own pack contained camera equipment and a drone, all for the making of videos for their YouTube channel! Carmelita told us that the Camino had been on her bucket list for some years ever since she'd watched *The Way*.

Lunch for us that day was bread and cheese and tomato, brought with us and eaten at a picnic bench with a spectacular view over the ocean. And we both took a little siesta too! We had completed our 15 km to Portecelo by the early afternoon. It's a small village with mountains to one side and sea on the other. It brought back good memories of Barmouth in Wales where we go on holiday every year in August. We found our apartment, 'Loft Peregrinos' and were welcomed most warmly by a local woman who wanted to tell us about everything. And she really did provide everything for us. There was a mouth-watering array of food and snacks and drinks. She explained that there would be no cafés on the way to Baiona and urged us to take as much food as we needed. She was so lovely and seemed so happy to be doing her bit to help weary pilgrims. She told us her name was Alicia. She was touched to hear that it was the name of my mum, also the second name of our daughter.

As well as the urging to eat lots of her food, Alicia told us of the various health benefits of sea water, especially for battered feet! We followed the short path down to the rocky cove and bathed our feet. I then went all the way into the water and was pleasantly battered again by the waves.

I woke in the morning, as usual, to the sound of the birds and stepped outside in the dark to hear the added pleasing noise of the waves crashing against the rocks down below. It was Day 6 on the Camino. And, I reflected, it was another day in paradise! Even if I'd had a fitful night's sleep and my body felt a bit beaten up and my first thought on waking was a tricky work issue. Even with all of that, it was a gift to be there, and to be there with Yim Soon, and to receive a daily dose of friendliness and kindness from those we met on the way, whether fellow pilgrims or locals.

We had strolled up to the bar/restaurant the evening before. We'd sat outside on the terrace and had ringside seats over the Atlantic. There was some fun with the ordering of our squid and chips and there was some lovely banter throughout, mainly in Spanish, with the women who served us. We were absolutely stuffed by the end, which gave me the ideal opportunity to try out my new Spanish expression on one of the women, "*Nos hemos puesto las botas,*" which translates literally as 'we have put on our boots!' I couldn't quite catch all of her reply but she was clearly delighted by my use of a colloquialism to denote that we'd really enjoyed the food and eaten lots of it! In general, I had made good use of my Spanish on our first day in Spain, including with Alicia at the apartment and I was reminded again of how much it's worth making an effort with other languages.

The dirt path from Portecelo followed the coastline and before long we caught up with Carmelita and James. Carmelita was walking better and looking much happier after a good night's sleep, and I was touched when she said that she'd been watching some videos of me on YouTube! I told them about the song I'd written after my first stage on the Camino Francés, *El Camino*, and they asked if they could use it in one of their videos. I said it would be a pleasure. James decided that it would be a perfect spot to launch his drone and we stayed to see how it all worked. He extracted a couple of bags from his pack and after a few minutes his so-called 'drone baby' was airborne and making a video of the stunning, rugged coastline. When he'd got it all packed away again I tried to pick up his rucksack weighing 18 kgs. It was extremely heavy! I couldn't imagine carrying that on its own, let alone that of Carmelita on top of it. Some people really do have heavy burdens to carry on the Camino!

We passed through the old village of Oia, famous for the Royal Monastery of Santa María de Oia. On our way along the main street I exchanged a few words with an old woman who said she didn't have to go travelling because she met the world in her village! Then when we stopped in the local café for a *café con leche* I chatted a bit with the young woman at the counter who, like Alicia the day before, was thrilled that I was having a go with the Spanish. I managed to explain to her that the experience of travelling and meeting people from all over the world is interesting; with other languages it is even more interesting. She nodded in agreement.

My next encounter with a local woman occurred when I was sitting for a quick rest outside a house. The owner appeared and asked if I wanted some water. I replied that I had enough but she was very kind. We got talking. Her name was Candida and she was seventy-two and had worked hard for forty years doing some kind of job (I couldn't quite understand what) at the coast and in all weathers. It sounded like her husband of forty-seven years had begun to develop dementia ten years previously and she was on her way to cook lunch for him in the care home where he now lived. She said to me repeatedly that it was important to enjoy life. She had a face that was etched with kindness, and indeed joy.

Soon after my meeting with Candida we got talking to Rob, a South African who had been living in Melbourne for fifteen years. When I'd greeted him he'd had to take out his earphones. He'd been listening to Prince Harry's book for four hours (each to their own!) and said he was glad to have a break from it. I asked what had brought him on the walk. He explained that eight years before, someone had given him a book about the Camino which had sat on his coffee table unread. He had extra holiday to take in 2023 and decided that now was the time. "It lures you in," he said of the experience, and went on to say, "there's something about this damn Camino that's just magical. It's really spiritual. You have to slow down and you see things." He thought there was something highly significant about the fact that people had been walking on these paths for hundreds of years. He agreed with me as well that there was something about the act of walking that brings out people's stories.

A few kilometres had sped by nicely whilst speaking with Rob. As we arrived back down at the sea he continued on and Yim Soon and I sat against a wall and enjoyed our lunch of cheese and ham sandwiches, courtesy of Alicia. And that was followed by a little siesta in the sun, with the sound of crashing waves a few meters away. It was not too far away at all from paradise.

For the final few kilometres into Baiona we followed the alternative green route around a peninsula by the side of the road. As with the day before, a few cars and motorbikes beeped their horns and there were friendly waves for us. I had the impression repeatedly that the Camino touches not just the pilgrims but also those who live in the places it passes through. And those local people touch the pilgrims in turn so that there is a virtuous circle of kindness.

After what seemed like an age we were on the outskirts of the city of Baiona. The sun was beating down, there was no shade anywhere and we'd run out of water. We found a slightly run-down road-side bar. We had a cold beer, and I chatted a bit with the young woman who served us. We were her only customers. It was Mothers' Day in Spain and it seemed that everyone had gone on that Sunday afternoon to rather more upmarket establishments. For me it was another precious encounter on the Camino. And the young woman seemed to enjoy the interaction too.

We finally made it into the historic centre of the town which is dominated by an almost perfectly preserved fortified castle on a promontory next to a large, modern marina filled with yachts. The reward for that day's long walk was a grand apartment with a balcony overlooking one of the narrow streets that were thronged with people on that Sunday evening. We found a church for a 7 p.m. Mass and I was rather tickled to hear through the open doors the roars of the crowd from a local football match just across the square. There was more entertainment later in the form of people playing the gaita, the Galician version of the bagpipes! It was yet another occasion when our pilgrimage was taking us right into the heart of the country and its culture.

At the end of Day 7, I was on the receiving end of more kindness, and I hoped I'd been able to give a bit of the love back! After the 25 km from Baiona we finally made it to the Hotel Bahia de Vigo which is right next to the harbour in that, the largest city on the Portuguese Camino. Our eighth-floor room had a fantastic view over the bay and it had a bath with a jacuzzi! We had earned it! After my bit of spa treatment I went down to the foyer to get a coffee and to write. One of the women on reception directed me to a café across the road where I ordered, with great excitement, a cup of black tea to take away. I was slightly dismayed when the young guy gave me a cup of hot water with a tea bag placed next to it (I'd thought it was only the French who committed such crime in the making of tea!). I acted swiftly and got the tea bag into the hot water and I even had time to let it steep. Then I asked if there was any cold milk. There was! And the guy went on to give me a piece of cake on the house. I was on cloud nine. And despite the unpromising start it was a great cup of tea.

Such, in a way, had been the day. It had started well enough. I woke with the first birdsong and went out to stroll along the attractive marina in Baiona. Yim Soon and I were on the road at 6.45 a.m. which meant that due to Spain being an hour ahead of Portugal it was still dark. We were rewarded for our early start with a beautiful red sky over the bay and the mountains on the other side. We eventually crossed over the estuary along an ancient stone bridge and we were back to following those yellow arrows. With it being Day 7 of walking I was feeling a bit weary and not really relishing the thought of the 26 km to Vigo. We got chatting to Emily from the States and had breakfast with her in the next town. Our salmon and avocado toasties, orange juice and *café con leche* fuelled us nicely but by now the sun was up and it was a case of head down and one foot after the next.

The day's recommended route was inland through pine and eucalyptus forest and it went up and down, up and down. Every now and again we got a glimpse of the view, right across the bay to some outlying islands. It was truly breathtaking. At one point in

71

the woods we met two women, one from Holland and her friend from Brazil. The former explained to me that coming on the Camino was an opportunity to weigh up some important decisions she had to make about her life. It seemed that she was slowly but surely coming to some clarity.

We emerged from the forest and were back on the roads. And from then until the end of the route the encounters with the pilgrims came thick and fast. At a passport 'stamping station' by the side of the road we met Rievis from Latvia who was looking fresh as a daisy despite having done some 40 km days and being only on Day 6 from Porto. I wasn't entirely surprised when he told me that his motivation for walking the Camino was sport and endurance!

Then Jitka appeared, the woman from the Czech Republic who had been the only other passenger with us on the speed-boat over to Spain. That day she had appeared rather subdued and had been walking slowly. Today she was smiling radiantly. She was a person transformed. Another Camino miracle! She had mentioned to us as well that being on the Camino gave her a chance to think about things. Sometimes those things were good, sometimes difficult. I reassured her that I had been having an argument with someone in my head earlier on in the day!

Then there came along two guys I'd spotted the previous evening in Baiona who looked like father and son. They were indeed father and son; and Preben and Stefan, I was excited to hear, were from Denmark. It was a first chance to pull out some of my Danish from thirty-five years before and they were suitably impressed. We left them so we could go into a local café for juice and more toast. I thought I'd chosen strawberry jam to go on the toast. It turned out to be tomato, to spread on the toast together with olive oil. It was a different way to take toast and it was actually very tasty.

Shortly after lunch we came across a group of six men of a certain age, most of them from Northern Ireland. A few had walked several Caminos together and in 2019 they had started in Lisbon and reached Baiona. The intention was to return in 2020 and continue to Santiago. COVID put paid to that and this was their first day back on the Camino. They were great company and it was sad to go our separate ways when we came into Vigo. One of the group, Colm was interested to hear that my mum had grown up in Newry. He was from Rostrevor himself and had gone to school in Newry. We were sure that we would know people in common, and I told him the story of how on my first Camino in 2015 I had met a Spanish man who was married to a Newry woman who knew my Uncle Pat. And how, whenever I meet anyone from Newry they invariably know someone who knows Pat!

Day 8 was the one where we cheated a bit! We'd got the idea of taking a train from Vigo from Christian and Mirjam. There was one leaving at 9.13 a.m. and it would take twelve minutes to reach Redondela, rather that the few hours required to walk the twenty odd kilometres! We'd also be able to have a big breakfast at the Hotel Bahia, which, I was excited to hear from the friendly Portuguese waiter the night before at the sushi restaurant, was where the Celta Vigo football team stayed before their home games. That meant we ate breakfast in the same room where a first division Spanish side have their pre-match meal! I wasn't feeling great, however. I'd awoken to grey skies and drizzle outside, my head was filled frustratingly with work-related worries, and I couldn't quite face another long day of walking and carrying my rucksack. I also got stressed when it looked as if we might miss our train. We didn't! There was a nice interaction with the woman at the ticket office, so too with the young women who were sitting next to us in the carriage. I finally began to relax.

There was a bit of a hike from the station at Redondela to the Camino trail, and by the time we were following the yellow arrows again it was raining. Just then a couple covered in tattoos came up behind us. I greeted them and we got chatting and it emerged fairly quickly that Sören and Melanie were walking the Camino for their honeymoon. We spent most of the morning together and heard about their business in Hannover which was a tattoo shop and other artistic pursuits! It was good that we could treat them to a coffee en route. I explained that Yim Soon and I had received much kindness on our honeymoon hitchhiking in the Lake District and we were happy to offer a little kindness in return.

It was great to walk and talk but we were moving a bit slowly so Yim Soon and I increased the pace a fraction. And soon after leaving the honeymoon couple we spotted a couple with a baby on the man's back. They were also from Germany and little eleven-month-old Otto was looking very pleased to be on the Camino. The man asked what had changed for me since my first Camino and I said it had been a time of seeing little miracles every day and coming to the realisation that those little miracles are probably happening around us all the time if only our eyes and ears and hearts are open.

I asked him the same question and he replied, "We got engaged yesterday!" He added, "The sun was shining and we were on the Camino and I thought that Otto would approve!" We were so happy for them. Another Camino miracle!

We had taken a couple of rolls and some cheese from the hotel in Vigo and we also had some strawberries and peaches that Yim Soon had bought in a greengrocer on the way. We shared them with Edmund from Latvia who was sitting at a picnic bench next to a bridge over a stream. The sun was glistening through the trees after the rain of earlier and it felt pretty close to paradise. For Edmund, as for many, the Camino was an opportunity to get away from the stress of 'normal' life and work and, also like many, the act of walking led to a certain clarity of thought. We were joined by a very colourful and artistic character from Poland called Edyta. She told us about her, unsuccessful sounding, time studying in Canterbury and about her, unsuccessful sounding, relationships. She went on to say that when buying her ticket for the taxi speedboat to Spain she had been offered a job for a few months as the ticket-seller! I thought that seemed like a nice little position, helping pilgrims across the river. Yim Soon wasn't so sure.

There were far more people on the Camino that day. In the same way that many Spanish begin the Camino Francés in Sarria because of it being just over 100 km to Santiago (and therefore qualifying them for their *Compostela* certificate), so too about half of those on the Portuguese Camino start at Tui for the same reason. This stretch is also where the Central Way joins up with the Coastal route. The influx of new pilgrims included a large contingent of

Spanish schoolchildren. Some of them were really struggling with the walking! Nevertheless, most were happy to call out 'Buen camino!'

After what seemed like an eternity we were finally just a few kilometres away from Pontevedra. And there was a choice of route. It was just at that point that we met Sneha and Julie, who both live in Australia. They told us that the green route to the left was a bit further than the yellow to the right but went through woods and alongside a river. What's more, Sneha, whose family were from Kerala, had the John Brierley guide to the Camino Portuguese. The next day, Yim Soon and I would be veering onto the 'Spiritual Way' and none of the phone apps included this section. Sneha showed me the relevant pages in Brierley and I gratefully took photos. I then explained that just before leaving on this Camino I'd had a book published with the title 'The Universe Provides.'

Sneha and Julie were good company with whom to go the final 5 km of the day. And on the way through the woods they spotted an elderly man they'd met the previous day. He was sitting on a rock and saying that he wished a taxi could come and pick him up! I could hear from his accent not just that he was Danish but that he was from Jutland. Wagner was most impressed when I explained, in Danish, that I'd once had a girlfriend who lived in Jutland. He was from Horsens himself, which is indeed in Jutland!

Pontevedra is yet another beautiful, historic town with narrow streets in the centre, attractive medieval churches and a large square around which are colonnaded buildings. Our hotel, Virgen del Camino, was right on the Camino. And it had a balcony. Which was perhaps all the more precious as I wasn't expecting it.

As I'd done on the previous day in Vigo, I went to a café and asked for a cup of tea with cold milk and was richly rewarded. Sneha had earlier bemoaned the lack of a decent cup of tea on the Camino so I told her two Camino tea stories. The first concerned my friend James. He had turned up to meet me in St-Jean-pied-de-Port in 2015 with a stove and a billycan in his rucksack; whilst I, following his request, had a packet of real tea in mine. That meant we were able to have a proper cup of tea every day, and in some very beautiful places. The second story was a bit less spectacular but no less special. It was that cup of tea, complete with free cake, in Vigo. I was able to send her an email later explaining that I'd got yet another good cup of tea, this one with a free biscuit. And that I'd pushed the boat out and asked for a second one!

It was time, then, to collect Yim Soon and follow those yellow arrows into the old town where we found a restaurant which was open at 8.20 p.m. (many restaurants in Spain don't open till 8.30!). We decided to go mad and ordered a litre jug of sangria and sat and drank and ate out on the terrace. There were no other customers and the waiter was keen to chat with us. I'm not really sure what was so funny but our part-English, part-Spanish conversation was punctuated by laughter. It was such fun. He was telling us, in part, of all the climbing we would have to do the next day on the way to Armenteira.

The garrulous waiter wasn't exaggerating about the climbing, but Day 9 was a great day of walking. We took the free breakfast at the hotel and were walking by 8.20 a.m. There were lots of pilgrims on the road, especially Spaniards who had begun at Tui. But 3.2 km out of the town, as foretold in the John Brierley book, the path split. The majority of people went right. For the 'Spiritual Way' it was left. Then, as we'd been informed the night before, we were into lovely, wide open countryside filled with vineyards, with views over to the sea; and with the path going up and down, up and down. At the top of one of the climbs we met our first other people on the Spiritual Way, two Dutch women. One of them explained how twelve years before she'd been visiting the Cathedral in Santiago and had been so moved by the sight of the pilgrims arriving and embracing one another and breaking down in tears. One day, she said to herself, she had to come and find out for herself what it was all about. Her dog walking friend from home was a willing companion.

After chatting a bit as well with Dominic, a young Polish-Spanish man doing his first Camino, we arrived at the grand old monastery at Poio, and decided to pay the small entrance fee to have a look around. I especially liked the main cloister. At the centre of it was a large fountain, with the rejuvenating sight and sound of running water. The church too had an atmosphere of peace and prayerfulness, created no doubt by the hundreds of years of daily prayer services that have taken place there.

From Poio we came back down to the shoreline, to the small town of Combarro. We had a *café con leche* and rested and looked out at the beautiful bay. When we started walking again we saw lots of *hórreos*, the little stone storage houses that are built on stilts and which I'd enjoyed seeing on our previous pilgrimage to Santiago. And then the yellow arrows pointed abruptly right, away from the sea, and it was up, up, up. As our waiter in Pontevedra had warned us, it was very steep and it was like that for most of the remaining 10 km to Armenteira.

At the top of the steepest section we were pleased to find a donation drink place, so too some other pilgrims and we began to chat as we sipped our cool juices. Andrew and Anne were a couple from near Melbourne, and they were with their Australian friend Ed, and Dave from Ohio, who they'd met on the Camino Norte the year before.

The dirt path kept on going up and up. It took us through more eucalyptus forest, and eventually we emerged in the village of Armenteira at the end of the 22 km hike from Pontevedra. It was just after 2 p.m, and the monastery was closed for siesta till 4.30. Luckily a restaurant was open and was serving pilgrim dishes. We both had egg and chips, with chicken and salad. And a very cool Galician beer. The others arrived in dribs and drabs: the Australians, the Dutch pair, some that we didn't know. Everyone got a little round of applause. It had been quite a feat of endurance to hike up the mountain, and following as it did several days of long walks. Edmund from Latvia also appeared from the woods and joined us. We spoke more about our motivations for walking, and I was touched when he declared to us that he was hoping to become a better father to his three daughters. The reasons why people decide to walk on the Camino are as multiple and varied as the pilgrims.

We had made it to the monastery! It's right up in the hills and is home to a community of nine Cistercian nuns. I was excited to be spending two nights there. We wandered over when the doors opened at 4.30 and were warmly welcomed by Paula the guest sister. As often is the case, however, I was initially a little disappointed: on this occasion by the fact that our room in the guest wing was one of the few that didn't have a balcony! What to do? What I *did* do was to go to the dining-room which did have a balcony and open the doors wide and look out over the monastery walls to the hills in the distance.

I was back in my spot by the balcony doors in the dining room the following morning at 6.30 a.m. after sitting outside in the courtyard for my morning prayer as dawn was just beginning to break. I was delighted to hear the tooting of an owl in the trees. All was silent, except for the buzzing of the overhead light. I was pleased that we didn't have to pack our rucksacks and set off to walk a ridiculously long distance. It was a day to go slowly and to rest.

I had been pleasantly surprised to enter the chapel the evening before and find it packed with pilgrims. They were presumably staying in one of the *albergue*s in the village and had come for Vespers, evening prayer, at 7 p.m. followed by a pilgrim blessing read in different languages. It was like many such occasions on the Camino Francés. Until then, we'd not seen more that about half a dozen people on the paths at any one time. Now there were a good fifty gathered together; pilgrims of all ages and nationalities. When the blessing was read in English by a Canadian woman I was almost in tears:

May the light and love of God bless and direct your steps.
May the roads rise up to meet you.
May you open your heart to silence. And keep with gratitude the joyous remembrance of the good things that you have encountered.
May God carry you in his hands to the arms of St James in Santiago.
And may you go back to your home full of light and joy.

This same woman was the only other person making a two-night stay in the guest house. The three of us sat together in the dining room for the 9 o'clock meal and chatted about our Caminos. Beth was an Anglican priest from near Toronto, and like us she had previously done the Camino Francés and had started the Portuguese leg at Porto. We discussed the spiritual aspect of the

Camino. For Beth this had become most apparent during her time in the monastery, joining the sisters for their services and coming together with other pilgrims on both evenings for the prayer and blessing.

We had an entire wing of the guest house almost to ourselves. The big old building had been carefully and tastefully restored and the very stones emanated a sense of peace and prayerfulness. As indeed, perhaps, do the stones of an ancient pilgrimage route like the Camino. I'd been discussing with Beth over our meal of fish and potatoes and beans what, if any, the difference was between a pilgrimage route and a long-distance walk. I mentioned the conviction of a couple I know that it is about intentionality. In other words, most people are undertaking the walk because consciously or unconsciously they are seeking something and are open to some kind of inner transformation. I told Beth about the tough first day's walk from Porto: in the heat, with a rucksack, and along a very touristy sea front. I'd asked myself why I was subjecting myself to such punishment and was afraid that it was 'just' a long-distance walk, albeit in a place with spectacular scenery. The spiritual aspect had crept up on me gradually. It came with the encounters, both with fellow-pilgrims and with the locals, where we shared our stories; and it became more and more apparent that some people were carrying a painful story. We all seemed to become a little bit more open as the days went by. As Craig the prison chaplain had said to me about his experience on the Camino Francés, there is a kind of stripping away that takes place. And as he said as well, it is hard *not* to have a spiritual experience.

For me, the beautiful location is also important for I believe that creation is to be enjoyed. To hear the hooting of an owl, or the crashing of the waves on the rocks; to look down from a hillside track and see the sun glistening on the bay; to revel in a sunrise or a sunset. This was very much part of the spiritual experience for me. I was reminded of the Jesuit writer and long-distance walker Gerry Hughes who is mentioned in later chapters. He said he imagined God asking him just one question when he died: "Did you enjoy my creation?" During all of my walks on the Camino, it was difficult not to.

79

I explained to Beth that part of the significance of a pilgrimage route was that people may have been walking along it for hundreds of years: just as South African Rob had said as well a few days earlier. All of those people, with all of their stories, with all of their blisters, with all of their different moods and life circumstances. All of us made equal somehow in the simple but profound act of putting one foot in front of the other. All of us on a journey to a place with a particular spiritual association. All of us with the opportunity to open our eyes and our ears to the beauty around us in the place, and in the people alongside us. And, as Melanie the tattoo artist insisted, to say thank you for all of the little miracles, and for the multiple ways that the universe provides each and every day.

It was a thoroughly restful day at the monastery, and we even ended up with a room with a balcony, albeit in slightly odd circumstances. Yim Soon had been badly bitten in the night and we discovered in the morning that her bed was infested by what I assume were that scourge of pilgrims through the ages, bed bugs. Sister Paula was most apologetic and moved us to a room that was bigger than the original and, my dream come true, had a balcony. There was a great view besides!

We joined the sisters for all of their services in the chapel, except the 5 a.m. Vigils. We ate good hearty meals in the guest dining-room. And we went for short walks in the afternoon. Even going just half an hour and with no rucksack to carry felt like a big effort! But it was a day to be gentle with ourselves, and to sink into the silence and the ancient monastic rhythms. On the way back from our afternoon stroll we spotted Jitka at the restaurant where we'd eaten lunch the day before. We embraced and chatted for a bit. We were also able to give her details of the boat company for the Saturday trip, for which she was grateful.

The chapel was full of pilgrims again for Vespers at 7 p.m. followed by the pilgrim blessing in the different languages. On the way out we met our second Korean pilgrim of the trip and what a character he was. His five Caminos to date had included one that began in Seville in the South of Spain and took ninety days to Santiago. He'd also done the Francés twice, and the Norte which he said was very hilly. He had been walking a lot on this trip with Juan from Barcelona who he described as his best friend! He was excited that I could speak Korean and when I asked him his name he replied, "Europe name, Al Pacino; America name, Donald Trump; Korea name, Mr Chon or John!" There followed a big photo session in the monastery courtyard, accompanied by much laughter. It was a lovely end to our day at the monastery, although it hadn't quite finished. We chatted warmly with Sister Paula when she brought us our meal, and then there was Compline in the chapel, the final communal prayer of the day. Our day at the monastery was well and truly complete.

I slept deeply in our new room with a view. I was awake at 6.20 a.m. and went outside as dawn was just beginning to break. Once again we went to the 7.30 a.m. Lauds and Mass in the Chapel. We had breakfast with Xavier who was at the monastery to do some electrical jobs. Then we said goodbye to Paula and we were walking again. After our very restful stay at the monastery and with it being our second last day of walking there was a new spring in my step as we passed along the flowing streams and little waterfalls that led us gently back down the mountain. Our Day 11 hike of 23 km to Vilanova de Arousa was very accurately called 'The water walk.' On the way through the woods we met a local man, José who was out for a stroll. He was delighted that I could speak some Spanish and told me with glee how his daughter had met her English husband whilst studying in Oxford. A bit further on we met three women from Blackpool. On a previous trip they had reached Burgos on the Camino Francés but had decided to do the Camino Portuguese this time, starting at Tui.

When we emerged from the woods we were on minor roads and on one such we came to a little chapel. There was a couple called Kathy and Tim inside giving stamps and they introduced us to an elderly Spanish gentleman, Don José. Concerned at the lack of chapels for pilgrims to visit, Don José had built the chapel ten years previously with his son, and named if after St Peter. Don José, it turned out, was ninety-seven. Continuing in the good and ancient tradition of old pilgrims returning to help new ones, Kathy and Tim had walked the Camino the previous year and were now spending six weeks on, as they put it, 'a mission.' Part of that mission was singing to visitors to the chapel, so that Kathy took a guitar and sang a song she'd written which was inspired by her stay at Armenteira. It was lovely, with the lyrics encouraging us to open our eyes to all that is around us.

I asked Kathy if I could sing a Camino song as well and took the guitar and sang the song I'd written eight years previously after my first stage. 'El Camino' was duly performed to Kathy and Tim, Yim Soon, a couple of women from California who were filming me, and Don José. There was a great acoustic in the chapel, although I was disappointed that I couldn't remember all the words.

At a late lunch stop we each enjoyed a delicious cheese and ham toastie and got chatting to Dirk from Belgium. Like Kim, the Korean we'd met at one point, Dirk was seventy-two and he had started in Lisbon. It was his Day 24 of walking and he said that his feet and legs were fine but he was mentally tired and just wanted it to finish. He was a veteran Camino walker and had now done all of the routes on the Iberian Peninsula. It all began for him many years ago when a well-known Belgian journalist used to give regular broadcasts about his time on the Camino Francés. Sadly when he and his wife were driving back through France afterwards they were involved in an accident and his wife died. Her funeral in Antwerp was attended by hundreds of people. Dirk decided that he would walk the Camino as soon as he retired. That was in April 2011; in May 2011 he set off from St-Jean-Pied-de-Port. He told me that he usually likes to walk alone and so the Camino Francés was far too busy for him. In the subsequent years he did all of the less-popular routes, and also learnt Spanish.

In 2022 he had begun from Seville in the South of Spain, which was over 1,000 km to Santiago. On the first stretch to Córdoba he had stayed with a little international group that included a Portuguese man, Antonio de Vaza, who cooked delicious meals for everyone in the evening. On his way from Lisbon in 2023 Dirk was pleased to visit that man in Braga, which is just North of Porto and on the pilgrimage route down to Fatima. He was also excited to hear that the man was president of the Portuguese Camino Association!

Dirk told me that he wasn't a Christian but that walking and being out in nature was a spiritual experience for him. It also gave him a chance to think, especially about challenging things that had happened for him earlier in life. He added that being on the Camino reminded him that there was good in the world.

After about 18 km we could see the water again and the final stretch for that day was along a windy coastline and into the seaside town of Vilanova de Arousa. We found our accommodation easily, a room in a simple but agreeable house called 'Pension Mar de Rosa' and were warmly welcomed by a local woman, Yolanda who announced proudly that the shellfish in Vilanova were the best in the world!

It was our final evening before Santiago. We went to the information bureau to find out where to take our boat in the morning and had a friendly exchange with the woman there. She told us where to go and also directed us to a bar in the town where we might be able to get an early breakfast. Café Jardim was on a square which was filled with young children running around, whilst their parents had a Friday evening drink with tapas on the outdoor tables. Having established that the café did indeed open at seven in the morning we joined the locals for a beer and some little free dishes. On our walk back down the main street we bumped into first Jitka, then Juan from Barcelona, then the three women from Blackpool, and finally Dirk on his way to a hidden away Portuguese restaurant. He invited us to join him and we happily accepted. The evening was finished off nicely by a walk around the harbour and a gorgeous sunset over the hills on the other side of the estuary.

I woke as dawn was breaking on our Day 12 which was to be a memorable final day to Santiago. We met Dirk in the café at 7 a.m. for breakfast then walked down to the port, which was packed with pilgrims waiting for a variety of small boats to Padrón. The one we had booked was announced and we climbed in. There were about ten passengers which included an Italian couple we'd passed a few times on the route, a Dutch couple, Dirk from Belgium and two guys in shorts with thick Dublin accents and one of whom had a variety of Camino tattoos on his legs. The Italian couple had, like us, been married for thirty years and they told Yim Soon how their daughter is into K-Pop and K-dramas and they knew how to say 'I love you' in Korean!

Just as the boat left the harbour at Vilanova, Jimmy (he with the tattoos) explained that his granddaughter Bonny Rae was making her first Holy Communion that day in Co. Wexford and he wanted to get a video of us all singing 'Let it Be' to send to her. A recording of the international choir was duly made and sent. It was very moving, and there was clearly something special about these two Dubliners sitting across from us on the boat. We had been told to take an extra layer of clothing and we could have done with a few extra layers because, once the little speed boat was out into the wide estuary it was absolutely freezing.

The boat stopped every now and then for a local woman to give some commentary and to point out the many crosses that had been erected on the banks of the river and in the little islets. At a certain point she told the story of how St James the apostle had arrived in Galicia soon after the death of Christ in order to preach the gospel; then following his martyrdom in Jerusalem how his disciples had come down this same estuary with his bones which they laid to rest in Santiago. Jimmy added the bit about King Alfonso II of Asturias doing the first Camino in about 820, which led to it being called the Camino Primitivo. I added the bit about the shepherd in the field seeing a star and that giving rise to the name Santiago de Compostela. The woman said she was impressed that we had done our homework about the story and thought it showed that we were not just tourists but true pilgrims on a faith journey! For me, it doesn't actually matter whether these stories are true in a historic, factual sense. To be sitting there in that boat with that fascinating collection of modern-day pilgrims, sailing down the very estuary that the disciples of St James are said to have sailed down and following in the steps of countless other pilgrims through the centuries in search of whatever it was they were in search of. That for me was an intensely powerful, and yes spiritual, experience.

An hour and a half later we were disembarking in Padrón. I walked with Jimmy and he told me his story. He had been an alcoholic but hadn't touched any drink in ten years. Six years previously he'd had in his Dublin taxi a young man who said he had just been on the

Camino de Santiago. Jimmy said to him, "Is that a cruise ship?" That young man sat in the taxi for two hours at his destination and told Jimmy all about the pilgrimage and Jimmy knew he had to go. He did the Francés in 2018 and had done a different Camino most years since then. In 2022 he had walked the Camino Ignaciano, a 640 km pilgrimage route first taken by Ignatius of Loyola, founder of the Jesuit order, from his birthplace in a village in the Basque country to Montserrat and Manresa. He had walked with a Jesuit priest called Brendan McManus who had written a book about it, and about Jimmy's story. The book is called *Brothers in Arms*.

My friend Tony, who happens to know Brendan McManus, had done the Camino Ignaciano when he was a Jesuit novice. He had set off in the summer of 1988 with another Jesuit novice, Chris, as it was the custom to walk in pairs. They caught the ferry from Portsmouth to Santander, then made their way to Loyola where the walk began. Tony was excited to be walking in the footsteps of St Ignatius and found the whole experience exhilarating. He and Chris could have taken with them a small amount of cash amounting to £2 each per day but they decided to take nothing and to be reliant on the generosity of strangers. They needn't have worried because the local people opened their homes to them, giving food and a bed. Some nights they simply slept outside or in church porches.

A short way into the pilgrimage Chris pulled a muscle so Tony had to walk alone which he loved. He felt, as he put it, "footloose and fancy free" and said it was a little bit like being a homeless person. He relished that opportunity to be completely reliant on providence. He observed that when you don't have anything, there's nothing to worry about! On the contrary, he had a sense of abundance.

Tony sees pilgrimage as a metaphor for life. For him life *is* a pilgrimage and he remarks that "Pilgrimage clicks you into how life really is."

A bit later on my walk from Padrón I walked with Dave. He is Jimmy's nephew, although just five years younger, and he also had some stories to tell about the ups and downs of his life. The year before, he had walked the first week of the Ignaciano with Jimmy and he had wanted to do the Portuguese as well with him. He said that walking on the Camino helped him to de-stress and to clear his head. He thought as well that his eyes had become a bit more open; to seeing flowers, for example. "I think it's making me a better person," he concluded.

Jimmy clearly loved to sing and we did another rendition of 'Let it Be.' He also sang a catchy song that an Australian called Dan Mullins has written about the Camino, 'Somewhere along the Way.' I sang, then, 'El Camino' and managed to remember the words this time. Dave was clearly touched and gave me a big hug. The songs continued a bit later on the path. Dave sang a song by Johnny Duhan made famous by Christy Moore, 'The Voyage.' He explained it was the song of him and Tina, his wife (who we'd both spoken to on the phone en route!). We followed that up by Yim Soon's favourite, 'When you were sweet sixteen.' Jimmy and Dave stopped after ten kilometres and we embraced and Yim Soon and I pressed on. We still had eighteen kilometres to walk. And there were lots more good encounters to come.

We caught up with the Dutch couple who had been on the boat, and they explained that it was the fifth and final stage of their walk which had begun in their home in Holland. Soon after that, I spotted in the rear distance a figure running and calling my name. It was Dirk who wanted to give me his email address so that I could let him know when my book about pilgrimage was published! Then I got chatting with Hanne and Jan from Copenhagen, who were delighted when I spoke to them in Danish. Hanne had been born in Slagelse, which was where I used to go to Mass when I lived in the country. Just as Dirk had done on a previous occasion, they had begun by walking the Mozárabe, so were coming to the end of their 1500 km which had commenced in Almería. They told me how hot and dry it had been in the South of Spain. They would be away from home for almost half a year and had rented out their house for that time. I was surprised to hear that they didn't have any problems with their feet, which seemed to have just sort of adapted and hardened to the daily pounding, including on a lot of cobblestoned roads earlier. Hanne had herself written a book about the Camino, and she also mentioned in passing a book she'd read in Danish about an

English couple who walk around the Cornish coast! I told her the story of Jörg. And here is part of Hanne's story.

…PILGRIMS' TALES…
Listen to the Way

Thousands of miles by foot on Europe's Camino trails with my partner, Jan have proven that a mindful and simple life surely exists and starts right outside one's front door. All it takes are some good shoes and the ability to pack the rucksack lightly. The first and most difficult step is to decide to do it. Then the Camino will provide and will show the Way.

So how can I implement everything I love about the Camino in my everyday life? Well, towards the end of our five-month walk, I ask the Camino to guide me. But one walking day leads to another without any reply. On the last day we arrive at a remote village in the South of France, where the daily bus is supposed to take us back to everyday life. Under the hot midday sun we wearily walk up and down the deserted main street, past closed shops, in search of a bus stop that evidently doesn't exist. As we are running short of ideas of how to get out of there, a middle-aged man in a faded pink polo shirt appears out of nowhere. I ask him for directions. In his explanation of where to wait for the bus he doesn't seem too certain, so I doubt whether he actually knows.

"You are a pilgrim," he then says. "You have to let go of control and listen to the people you meet on your way to Santiago. They each have a message for you." I object that I am on my way home and he repeats his message, now with such a powerful and knowing voice that, all of a sudden, he sounds like a very wise man. Maybe he's even the alchemist I had previously been hoping to meet, so I ask him what other message he might have for me. "Listen carefully, reflect and learn." And with these words, he walks away.

But then he turns back and looks me firmly in the eyes: "Don't try to control events, things or people. Be open, listen, reflect and then let go. Let life flow through you like a river. Be yourself. You are unique just the way you are."

Astonished by this unexpected encounter, I walk the last few hundred steps to the bus stop at a very slow pace, almost regretting that we can't continue our Camino now, as everybody on the Way obviously have a message for me.

At this point, there appear some of the faces of the people that we'd already met and they each have their message. "Stay in touch with the Camino soul by allowing more kindness and helpfulness in your life." "Watch, listen and learn" (this message had been delivered before!). "Evolve your talents and live your passion" (I'd heard that one several times). During a recent 'random' pilgrim meeting along a roadside I even became aware that I am the bridge or channel that will allow the Camino spirit to keep flowing, and Jan will remind me that 'to be or not to be' means to treat ourselves with daily moments of being rather than doing.

Sitting in the shadow under a big tree waiting for the bus I feel the inner peace that has agreed to accompany me wherever I go and hear that mature female voice that once told me that to grow we have to spend time with family and friends. I grasp the prayer written by an unknown woman that like yet another Camino miracle has found its way into my pocket. "Pray for my children that they will meet good people and for me to be a loving grandmother."

I resolve as well to keep on walking, and keep on listening…

Hanne, Denmark

A little later Yim Soon and I met yet another person who had written a book about his experiences of walking ridiculous distances. Henk and Barbara were a charming young couple. Henk was from Holland and Barbara from Mexico and they had first met in Cork! Henk also had Sam, his dog with him. Henk had walked the Camino Francés, then decided he needed something longer, so walked to Rome in ninety days, which included going across the Great St Bernard Pass in November in snow. He wanted something longer still so spent six months walking to Jerusalem. He decided to make that journey with no money and his story is told in Chapter 6. He said to me, "I love being around pilgrims." It was certainly great to be around him, and Barbara too and all of the countless other amazing people we had met. The next such were at a little portable café just a few kilometres shy of Santiago that had a laid-back vibe. We treated Henk and Barbara to drinks and as we sat down in the comfy chairs I spotted the couple with two children that I'd heard were on the Camino. They were Polish and they looked exhausted. I assured them that their little girl of three and their baby boy of eight months would be having an incredible experience which would leave an indelible imprint on their lives.

We left Henk and Barbara behind and we were finally on the outskirts of Santiago. Our room was on the way into town so we checked in before walking the last steps to the Cathedral. We went to the famous Plaza del Obradoiro where pilgrims have been arriving for hundreds of years. We gave each other a big hug. We had made it. The last time we'd stood in that square, six years before, the walls of the cathedral had been covered in scaffolding and the arrival had felt like an anticlimax. Pilgrims come to that place after their long journeys with such a range of emotions: elation and tears for some; maybe for others just sheer exhaustion. I was actually pretty happy to be there in that special place with this special woman who is my wife. And I wasn't too disappointed when we attended the 7.30 p.m. pilgrim Mass and there was no swinging of the *botafumeiro*. Neither was I overly bothered that, in contrast to six years before, I looked around at the crowds in the pews and recognised hardly anyone. Each experience is different and it would be unfair to say that one is any better than another. We walked away through the crowds and found a cheap and cheerful restaurant with a Pilgrims' Menu on offer. And we had an early night.

The centre of Santiago is almost eerily quiet in the early morning. I was glad to have the chance to be in the Cathedral with just a few other people, and there was an atmosphere of peace and prayerfulness. I followed the signs to go under the high altar to see the box wherein lie, supposedly, the bones of St James the apostle. Did St James really come to Galicia in the First Century? Did his disciples really carry his bones along the stretch of river we had sailed down ourselves the previous day? As said already, to me it didn't really matter! The whole of the Camino, so too the physical building which is the Cathedral, had been made sacred by centuries of people walking in faith; each of them carrying their particular hopes and burdens and stories.

I stood one last time in front of the ornate, golden screen behind the altar; and I said thank you: for that special journey I'd been on with Yim Soon, for all of the people we had met on the way. Then, needing the toilet, I went into a café and ordered a *café con leche*. As I took the first sip, in came the Australians we'd met on the way up the mountain to the monastery at Armenteira, Ed and Andrew and Anne. I told them about Jimmy, and about his book and his story. I mentioned that Jimmy had sung to us a song about the Camino by an Australian, Dan Mullins. They said Dan Mullins did a great Camino podcast and he had once interviewed them for it. It was another profound moment of encounter and connection on the Camino.

It wasn't over yet! After a late breakfast we found, with some difficulty, the office for getting the *Compostela* certificate. I'd begun to get a bit tense about finding our way through a now bustling Santiago, then got more stressed when I saw that before we could enter the building we had to scan a QR code and complete an online form; a form which would not accept Yim Soon's family name of Ku because it only recognised names with at least three letters! We got there in the end but my nerves were now jangling, and the final straw was queuing in the sun for ages to get into the Cathedral and then not being allowed in because it was full. I'd set my heart on going to the Pilgrims' Mass and seeing the *botafumeiro* again. I was deeply disappointed and was struggling to cope with the crowds of people and the constant, jarring noises everywhere. As is usually the case, I was finding it hard to make the transition from pilgrim to tourist.

We found a park and I lay in the grass for a while. And then returning through the vast Plaza del Obradoiro a young woman waved over at us. It was Jenny, who'd been walking with Jörg 1. She was lying down in the sun, resting on her rucksack and looking very pleased to have reached the end. And then we spotted the thirty years married Italian couple whose daughter likes K-pop and K-drama, and I imparted my very few words of Italian to them. I was coming back to life. We found a restaurant near the *Compostela* office and just as we were about to sit down at a table Hanne and Jan appeared. They joined us for the Pilgrims' Menu meal. And then there came along Henk and Barbara and Sam and there were more embraces. And a little later came Dave, wearing his familiar hat; with Jimmy, as was normally the case, thirty metres behind. There were more warm hugs. I was most touched when Jimmy told me that meeting us had made his week. I had also been deeply moved by meeting him and Dave.

Before the end of our meal with Hanne and Jan we were philosophising a bit about the 'magic' of the Camino. On this our latest pilgrimage I'd heard several reasons why people decide to do it. Hanne said simply, "We're walking for fun!" No doubt there's a bit more to it as well. A lot of people are in a lot of pain, with blisters and such like and I suggested that the pain was, in some mysterious way, an essential part of the experience. Jan agreed and said that such a long walk in such an unfamiliar place was a way to be taken out of one's comfort zone. Hanne added that it was good sometimes to have the experience of being vulnerable. And I mused that this meant we had to rely on others for help; also that there was a giving and receiving of basic human contact and kindness. I remarked again that the Camino touches as well the local people whose towns and villages are passed through by pilgrims: day after day, year after year, century after century. A constant, mutually enriching flow of kindness; of hearts being touched; of lives being transformed.

Quite a few of the wonderful people we had met on our Portuguese Coastal Camino were on Camino No. 6, No. 7, No. 8. I thought there was a good chance that Yim Soon and I would follow suit, and as we boarded the bus to take us to the airport I almost couldn't wait for the next one to start.

First, we were to walk on another ancient route but one a lot closer to home...

CHAPTER 4

CANTERBURY

Two weeks after our return from the Portuguese Coastal Camino, Yim Soon and I were setting off on another pilgrimage, this one that I'd heard about by chance.

In the bone dry summer of 2022, I had been out walking on the final stretch of the Pilgrims' Way to Canterbury. I had come to a notice board announcing that this was the spot where pilgrims would have got their first sight of the Cathedral, seven and a half miles away. The board also mentioned an annual pilgrimage from London to Canterbury over the May Bank Holiday weekend. It was organised by St-Martin-in-the-Fields Church in Trafalgar Square to raise funds for The Connection, a homelessness project next to the church. There would be three overnight stops in church halls en route; and it partly followed the old Pilgrims' Way.

I went home and told Yim Soon about it and on May 26th 2023, the feast day of St Augustine of Canterbury, we found ourselves and our sleeping bags (so too my guitar) in the courtyard of St Martin-in-the-Fields. There were seventy of us setting off to walk the seventy-four miles and there would be more of us by the time we reached Canterbury. We were welcomed and given a blessing by Sam Wells, rector of the church. He explained that there would be times on the way when we might feel discouraged and he cited St Augustine as an example. Augustine had been sent by Pope Gregory in 596 to bring Christianity to the Anglo-Saxons of Britain but when he and his monks reached France he got cold feet and returned to Rome, only to be sent back again by Gregory the following year. Even St Augustine got discouraged!

Group leaders had been assigned and we chose our group

according to pace. I opted for the quickest group. Yim Soon went for one of the slow ones on account of a sore knee, due to having to keep up with me a fortnight earlier on the Camino! Just before we left, we were reminded of the principal reason for the pilgrimage: to raise funds for The Connection. On the banner used for the first of many photo ops. were the words 'Walking to end Rough Sleeping in London.'

There were eight in my group, and we were as varied in personalities and backgrounds as a group can be. I was a bit unsure at first what I'd got myself into. There was one man who spoke incessantly, another who had his face covered with a scarf and didn't say anything at all, and a third who was wearing a superhero costume and whose only words seemed to be to tell others off if they were falling behind! 'Are these the people I'll be with day and night for four days?' I asked myself, rather uncharitably, and I even began to hatch a plan to change group the following day! But that's part of the rich experience of pilgrimage, and I would begin to connect with each person as the day wore on. Just like with Chaucer's pilgrims, a disparate bunch of characters had been thrown together on a long-distance walk. And by some miraculous, unexpected process those characters slowly but surely began to form into a little community.

I very much enjoyed the first part of the walk. It took us over the Thames via Hungerford Bridge and then along the bustling South Bank, with views across to St Paul's and the new City skyscrapers. The weather was perfect for walking, warm without being too hot and with the gentlest of breezes. At a certain point we veered away from the river and for several miles were going along busy London thoroughfares. As we came into the borough of Southwark I was excited to pass an intersection of Tabard Street and Pilgrimage Street. We were close to the site of the Tabard Inn where Chaucer's pilgrims set out from and, for a time at least as we went along the Old Kent Road, we were following exactly the same route that those medieval walkers would have taken. After five miles we came to All Saints church in New Cross and were rewarded with cups of tea and dishes filled with delicious Chinese food. I was relieved to see Yim Soon arrive just as my group was about to set off again and to hear that she was walking fine.

As I always find on pilgrimage, fascinating conversations are had, and sometimes they come as if from nowhere. So too are the most remarkable connections uncovered. Clarissa in my group had asked what had brought me and I told her about seeing the noticeboard at the point on the Pilgrims' Way near Canterbury where the Cathedral can be seen for the first time and reading there about a pilgrimage from St. Martin's. Clarissa mentioned that to Keith, our group leader, and he told me with pleasure that it was he who had conceived of the idea for that noticeboard. It had been designed and erected partly in memory of a man called Bob who was a veteran on the pilgrimage since its inception in 1990.

I spoke more with Clarissa later. The pilgrimage was a significant event for her and she had done it several times. She had often walked with family, including her daughters when they were younger, and the communal aspect was important for her. She also valued the daily services and the chance to be in a contemplative space. There's something as well, she thought, about the simple act of putting one foot in front of the other that brings our focus into the present moment. I was tickled that one of Clarissa's nephews, who had taken part as a young child, had been given a middle name of 'Pilgrim!' And another of her nephews was used as a model for the 'Christ Child' sculpture under the portico of St Martins.

John is another veteran on the walk and he was explaining how he dresses up as a different character every year. The year before he had been James Bond and on previous occasions a succession of superheroes. This time it was the red-suited Flash from the 1950s Marvel comics. It drew a lot of shouts from car windows as we made our way out of London. John told me how walking helps him to calm down and not lose his temper. I was touched by the bit of time we spent together in the afternoon when we were walking slightly in front of the others. I was likewise surprised when the 'silent' man, Yubarj from Nepal, told me he was covering his face not to avoid speaking to fellow pilgrims, rather to avoid inhaling tiny particles from the plane trees! I was even more struck by Yubarj's answer to my question of how he had first got involved with the pilgrimage. He had become homeless sometime after his arrival in London and had received great support from The Connection. He was one of two people in my small group, and several in the larger group, who had personal experience of sleeping rough. I met another of them at the end of the day when I was brushing my teeth in the toilets of the church hall.

Our afternoon stop was in the lovely Christ Church in Chislehurst, where we were welcomed with tea, sandwiches and cakes. I collapsed into a sumptuous settee in the bright and attractive atrium area, and the church itself had a warm and prayerful atmosphere. It even had, to my pleasant surprise, comfortable seats, the pews having been pulled out some years before. I had to prise myself out of the settee to walk again but just six miles remained and we were glad to be leaving the busy urban sprawl of London behind us. Eventually we found ourselves walking through woods and fields and those six miles passed quickly. We completed our nineteen miles for the day and were the first to arrive at the church of St Mary the Virgin in Swanley. There was more tea served by the team of volunteers, as well as a round of applause from them! It had been a good first day of walking.

I spent a pleasant hour sitting out in the graveyard in a gentle breeze and felt the unique satisfaction that comes from doing a really long walk. And I was well ready for the meal that was served in the church hall. I was pleased to see that the group included a couple with their young son and asked if I could sit with them. After we'd been chatting for a few minutes, Yim Soon appeared and it turned out that she'd walked with them during the day. "She's been telling us lots about you," Bobby exclaimed to me, "I feel as if I know you already." I enjoyed the time with Bobby and Beth and three-year-old Abraham, and they told the story of how they'd met and then asked Yim Soon and me to tell our story.

There were a couple of further treats in store for us. The vicar arrived and led us in Compline. This short and simple service has for hundreds of years been the final communal prayer in monasteries, and it's a peaceful and poignant endpoint to the day. As explained previously, its name literally means 'complete.' And then there came the cherry on the icing on the cake. A group of six men and women from St Martin's stepped forward holding music books and sang a piece by Thomas Tallis, 'If Ye Love me.' It was utterly sublime, and the day truly was complete.

Those who were not either staying at the Swanley Premier Inn or sleeping in tents in the vicar's garden remained in the church, having found a little nook or cranny for their sleeping bag. Yim Soon and I commandeered a row between pews! I didn't expect to get a lot of sleep but how wonderful it was to be there.

I woke as the first rays of light were appearing through the windows high up in the church. That meant that I had managed, despite lying in a thin sleeping bag (my Camino one: it was warmer in Spain in April than in London at the end of May!) on a hard floor and amidst a cacophony of noise, to get two or three hours' sleep. It was enough; it was more than enough. One of the realisations of pilgrimage is how satisfied we can be with so little. I got dressed and went outside and saw on a clock that it was just 4.30 a.m. I realised that we were right in the centre of Swanley. Whilst being in the county of Kent it is also part of the conurbation of London and close to the busy M25 motorway. It's probably not renowned as being the prettiest town in Britain but as I wandered its empty streets and listened to the birds and noticed the trees in leaf and spotted the long views over the fields towards the motorway, it was the most beautiful place in the world. 'Another day in paradise,' I said to myself.

When I got back to the church I saw that Kenny from my group was also an early-riser and he had already boiled the kettle. This meant that my next simple pleasure of the day was a cup of tea taken outside on a chair, looking out over the graves! It was still very early so I did what I'd done the previous evening. I took my laptop out to a bench in the graveyard and spent a most enjoyable hour writing. Back in the church the pilgrims were just starting to emerge, bleary-eyed, from sleeping bags. I find that there is something very intimate about waking up with people. As Danish Hanne observed, part of the pilgrimage experience is making ourselves a bit vulnerable, away from our usual routines and comfort zones. The time of waking and getting up can be a particularly vulnerable time for people.

We packed our temporary worlds back into our bags and were given the welcome news that breakfast was being served in the hall. To my pleasant surprise there was bacon and egg and beans and bread. It was a feast, and never have baked beans tasted so good! Just as the centre of Swanley had seemed beautiful to my pilgrim eyes, so a plate of baked beans was a banquet to my pilgrim stomach.

And then we were on our way for the twenty miles to Aylesford Priory, picking up some extra pilgrims at the station. My group was boosted by two old hands on the walk, Will and Mel, together with Mel's dog, Blake. I chatted with Will on the first section and he remarked how he enjoyed the variety of people encountered on a pilgrimage. Clarissa said something similar when she pointed out that the experience of walking, eating and sleeping together was 'a great leveller.' As we came over the old stone bridge leading into the picturesque village of Eynsford, Will told me he'd been doing the pilgrimage for about twenty years and he also explained that the origins were not just about raising awareness and funds for the homelessness project of St Martin's. Kath and Roger Shaljean were Quakers who had worked in that project for forty years and in 1990 in an effort to heal divisions within the church community they had the idea of everyone doing something challenging together i.e. going on pilgrimage! Kath's vision was just as Clarissa had discovered, that the communal act of walking, eating, sleeping, even going to the toilet, would unify people. It was also important for Kath and Roger that some of those who had been served by the homeless project should take a central part. As I'd discovered the day before, that was clearly still the case.

We were warmly welcomed by the parishioners of St Martin's, Eynsford and even though it was only 9.30 a.m. and I was still full from the cooked breakfast I couldn't resist the cakes on offer. I chatted with Kate and was interested to hear that she, like Yim Soon and I, had walked on the Rota Vicentina. It's a long-distance footpath along the rugged coastline of Southern Portugal and it's known in English as 'The Fishermen's Trail.' Kate was equally interested to hear that we had recently returned from the Portuguese Coastal Camino. I tried to explain what I thought might be the difference between a pilgrimage and a long-distance walk but was struggling to. Kate and I were to come back to that topic.

We bid a reluctant farewell to Eynsford and were going steeply uphill through large, open wheat fields. The reward at the top was fantastic views which can reach all the way to Canary Wharf on a clear day (it wasn't quite!). There was yet more tea and cake on offer at the next church stop, in West Kingsdown. Then it was back into the woods for another few miles. We were now close to the Pilgrims Way. This is claimed to have been the route taken for hundreds of years by those starting their Canterbury pilgrimage in Winchester, although this is disputed. We cut South into the village of Trottiscliffe where we had a feast of cold rice dishes for a late lunch. Getting up again for the final seven miles was a challenge.

We managed to keep going and finally we could spot the old monastery buildings on the opposite side of the Medway River. A couple had just got off the bus and they had bags and a vaguely pilgrim look about them! They were pilgrims indeed. It was Eddie and Wan from Hong Kong, friends of Eugene, one of the organisers. I walked with them along the bank of the river and then over the long, medieval bridge that brought us into the pretty village of Aylesford. They told me how they had come to London a year before, seeking a slower, calmer life.

The Carmelite priory at Aylesford is itself a place of pilgrimage, having at its centre a shrine dedicated to Mary as well as several little chapels dedicated to the saints of Carmel. The priory was founded in 1242 when the first friars arrived from Mount Carmel in Jerusalem, having been given a piece of land belonging to the estate of Richard de Grey, a crusader. An attractive tree-lined avenue leads down to the priory and we were greeted there by an exuberant sight. The trees were festooned with silver streamers and the grounds were filled with families from the Keralan Syro-Malabar community. Like us, they were there on pilgrimage. The women were dressed in colourful saris, drummers were drumming and there was a festive atmosphere. Probably the only walking they would have done during the day would have been around the field which, besides the silver streamers, displayed pictures of various saints, but it was a pilgrimage nonetheless. They had come to a holy place, they had taken part in religious ritual, and they were having a great time together and tucking into a delicious meal!

There was an evening service for our group in the Relic Chapel, which had beautiful, modern stained-glass windows that I loved to gaze at. The service was simple and prayerful and it was led by one of the Carmelite friars who gave us a definition of pilgrimage that was short and to the point and probably much better than the one I'd attempted to give Kate earlier in the day. "It's not just a journey," he said, "it's a bringing of our hopes and our dreams and our pains and our sufferings to a holy place." We heard once again the sublime voices of the little impromptu St Martin's choir singing in parts a sacred piece from the Tudor period, and I returned happily to the guest quarters of the priory for yet more food: Bar-B-Q chicken and salads. I spoke at the table with Alan who likes walking long distances and who said how he appreciates the aspect of 'slowing down,' also the encounters with people.

Yim Soon and I had taken the option, as had many, of our own room at the priory and that included the luxury of a shower! I woke in the morning having slept deeply but, initially, not really relishing yet another day of being in a large group and walking a very long distance. I strolled through the peaceful priory grounds, I happily accepted a cup of tea prepared by the refreshments team, I sat by the lake and listened to the shrieking of the Canada Geese. It felt good to be alive.

For the first few miles from Aylesford we followed a dirt track through large fields of wheat, oats and barley. These were replaced, in turn, by vast new vineyards. I reflected to myself that Chaucer's pilgrims would probably have been passing through hop fields; and no doubt they would in the evening have enjoyed a tankard or two of the ale made from those hops.

I was surprised to emerge from the fields onto the A249 at the place where there is a speed camera. I have many times driven along that busy dual-carriageway and slowed down at that very point. There's a sad story associated with this spot. When the road was built in the 1960s it divided the village of Detling in two. In 2000 a young girl called Jade and her grandmother had been killed while trying to cross the road to the other side of the village. Jade's parents began a campaign to have a footbridge constructed over the road and it was this bridge, named 'Jade's Crossing' which we went over to get to the village hall. We arrived in the hall to the sight of another morning feast: a variety of melons, sandwiches, thick slices of Victoria sponge cake, and scones. I was still pretty full from another cooked breakfast but I somehow found room for a few slices of melon, a piece of cake and a mini cream tea. And I had another interesting conversation with Kate, this time about the cultural identity of our children, due to her husband being Indian. I was fascinated as well to hear that Kate works as a doctor with the R.A.F. She was one of at least five medics in the group.

There was a welcome mixing up of the groups for the next stretch. I spoke with Emily who works at The Connection and was one of the organising team. We discussed what it is that makes a pilgrimage a pilgrimage. I told her that the day before, a friend of mine had attended a talk in Cambridge about pilgrimage. Victor and Edie Turner maintain that there are key elements of pilgrimage. The first is the aspect of liminality, namely being at a threshold or being between worlds. I mentioned to Emily that this seemed to correspond with the ancient Celtic belief in 'thin' places, where one can almost reach out and touch heaven. I had been in places on the Camino that I very much experienced as being 'thin.' Such places are sort of on the margins and the Turners contend that on pilgrimage we become in a sense marginal people. It is a tiny experience of being a nomad or even of what it is to be homeless. We are outside of our usual comfort zones and in a different space, and the most interesting things can happen in this space.

Victor and Edie argue as well that pilgrimage can act as a rite of passage; in the same way that many cultures traditionally sent their young away on some kind of spiritual quest. Finally, they note the importance of the communal aspect. You meet people you wouldn't normally meet and you end up having profound conversations with them. This was most certainly the case on this walk to Canterbury, so too on all such walks I've done.

I had a similar conversation a little later with Fran who was both one of the St Martin's singers and one of the doctors. I was excited to hear that she'd been to Taizé in the South of France and that she had travelled there by train from Copenhagen! Why not? She had done other long-distance walks, and she was interested in the Camino. I mentioned that Bobby, father of Abraham was, like her, a paediatrician. "He used to be my supervisor," she explained.

The pavilion at Hollingbourne was our venue for a ploughman's lunch. Hollingbourne is also the location of the Dirty Habit pilgrim inn dating from the 11th Century. This was the second place on that day's walk where medieval pilgrims would undoubtedly have stayed. The first was at Boxley, where an abbey once stood. An abbot of Boxley had been a friend of Thomas Becket and was one of those who buried the martyr in the cathedral after his death in 1170.

After lunch, we had eight miles to go along the Pilgrims Way, which doubles now as the North Down's Way. The path followed a ridge along the chalky hillside and there were more stunning views down over the valley. We arrived at Charing in the quaint old barn and I spoke again with Kate. Following our earlier conversation she'd also been asking people what they thought the difference was between pilgrimage and a long-distance walk. As I'd found myself on the Camino and elsewhere, those who weren't religious didn't really see any difference. In common with the conclusions of Victor and Edie Turner, Kate herself spoke about pilgrimage being a place of threshold and a turning point. For her, there was also a recognition that something has ended. That can be accompanied by some disquiet and there are echoes for her between the pilgrimage journey and transitions in life.

Kate agreed with me that pilgrimage provided a liminal space. She had a fascinating insight that while we walk together we have no past and no future. We have only a present. As with walking on the Camino we will in the majority of cases never see the person again. That possibly makes us more open, and more receptive to the seeds of ideas. Kate concluded that pilgrimage is "A little glimpse of heaven!"

I'm struck as well by how we see things on pilgrimage that we might not normally notice. I was touched to overhear Sean from my small group explaining with delight to somebody about "The sheer beauty of the countryside, the orchards, the wildflowers." This reminded me of Dave who I met on the Portuguese Camino telling me how he had started to notice the flowers at the side of the road.

There was a sublime time of prayer at 6.30 p.m. in the village church with Sandra the vicar. She had Taizé music playing before and after the service which almost had me in tears. So too when the St Martin's choir stood up and gave us a third piece of sacred music from the Middle Ages. And then it was time to eat, and what a feast we had in the barn: spicy Indian dishes followed by apple crumble. And that was followed by a popular Sunday evening tradition on the event, 'Pilgrims got Talent.' *What* a talented bunch we were: storytellers, poets and musicians. I was one of the last to perform and I sang 'El Camino,' and had a great violinist Chris to accompany me. I was then joined by Yim Soon for our Korean party piece *Sarangun onjena ku jariea*, love is always in that place.

When I'd taken a brief stroll earlier down the main street of Charing the owner of The Bookmakers Arms must have thought I had a pilgrim look about me because he asked me out of the blue, "Are there pilgrims in the village this evening?" I confirmed that there were and he said he hoped to see some of us later. We didn't disappoint, and having a drink in what looked like a converted shop was a nice end to the day. Yim Soon and I chatted with Chris and his fellow pilgrimage musician Alistair. They had done a couple of fantastic numbers in the barn. Alistair plays a mean slide blues guitar and one of their songs had been his own composition, 'Pilgrimage Blues.' Chris explained in the bar that he had done the first of his twenty-four Canterbury pilgrimages as a seventeen-year-old. At nineteen he was a group leader for the first time and it was the year that it rained torrentially for the entire four days. These things can happen on pilgrimage! We live to tell the tale, and there was Chris telling his tale over two decades later!

It was another sleepless night for me in my impromptu bedroom, which was the store cupboard in the village hall. I had to be up and alert at 5.45 a.m. to give my BBC Radio 2 *Pause for Thought*. That always induces some anxiety but it went well and I walked jubilantly back up the village street to the church and the barn in search of a cup of tea. It was too early! One of those on the pilgrimage who was himself homeless wandered up to me and asked if I'd heard the latest evidence about the authenticity of the Turin shroud. I said I hadn't and that I didn't want to hear about it just then! I've had some surreal early-morning conversations when on pilgrimage, especially on the Camino, but I decided to give that one a miss!

I was back at 7 for the final breakfast of bacon, sausage, eggs and beans. I was served my tea from the lovely ladies from Hong Kong and enjoyed some warm banter with them, so too with various others in the crowded barn. There was a definite 'end of term' atmosphere. I was full of gratitude for this experience and for this motley group of characters that I had shared it with.

We set off for the final seventeen miles to Canterbury. Some people had come down from London for that final day so that we were now a group of over one hundred making our way through the wheat fields beyond Charing. We continued on the Pilgrims Way as it followed its course along the gently sloping hillsides of the North Downs. There were still long, wide views in every direction. I asked Linda in my group what had been her favourite moment of the pilgrimage. She told me that when she did the first of her several pilgrimages she had walked across the long, stone bridge into Aylesford and had spotted a swan nesting on the riverbank. The swan had stood up and flapped her wings, as if to signal to passing pilgrims how proud she was of her egg. Linda had been delighted by that sight and remembers that moment fondly each year that she comes along that stunning bridge into Aylesford. She had also, as I had, enjoyed entering the priory and seeing the Indian group in their colourful clothes and the sound of the drums.

More tea and more cake awaited us at All Saints church at Boughton Aluph which is described as a 'Thirteenth Century pilgrims church.' A notable feature is the big old Tudor fireplace in the South porch, said to have provided warmth for pilgrims before setting off on the next stretch of their journey. The fire had been lit specially for us.

On the long stretch to Chartham we were into what for me is familiar territory: paths and roads where I've walked or cycled many times over the years. We came through the woods to the noticeboard where, the year before, I had learnt about the St

Martin's pilgrimage and from where the Cathedral can be seen in the distance. Group photos were taken, then we carried on and out of the woods and came into the quintessentially English village of Chilham. It was there that we deviated from the Pilgrims Way. Our target was St Mary's church in Chartham where we were met with a huge array of delicious cakes. And from there it was just four miles into Canterbury along the river Stour. Having not slept at all the night before, I was feeling exhausted and walked back quickly and on my own so that I could go home for a bath and a nap before the final service.

I re-joined the group at the Friends' Meeting House in the centre of Canterbury and we set off en masse at 6 p.m. to process to the Cathedral. We gathered in the crypt and were treated to the sublime voices of the whole of the St Martin's choir, the rest of which had travelled down from London just for the service. There were words of thanks for the organisers. Then there were reflections from two pilgrims. Peter was a client of The Connection, having been homeless himself. He spoke of how grateful he had been for the friendliness and kindness of everyone he had walked with. Patrick told of how in 1979 as an eighteen-year-old he had been invited to go on pilgrimage. When told that it was a religious journey involving a lot of walking and then sleeping at night on floors he politely declined. When told that it would include pupils from the local girls' school and that they would stop each lunchtime in a pub and then each evening in a pub he decided to do it! That was the first of countless pilgrimages he had taken part in, and he noted that both realities he'd been presented with are true of pilgrimage. The sacred and the profane have always gone hand in hand. Medieval pilgrims to Canterbury would, I'm sure, have enjoyed some ale and some entertainment along the way. And they would surely as well have been profoundly marked by their journey to the holy ground of the Cathedral. Patrick said that he had discovered what many have discovered, that pilgrimage is a place of transformation.

There was another great song from Alistair on his guitar and Chris on his violin. And then we processed, singing, into the cloisters where Dean David of the Cathedral placed flowers on the grave of Dick Shepherd. As rector of St Martin's when the First World War ended, Shepherd had welcomed homeless ex-soldiers, a ministry which led ultimately to the present day work of the Connection. The Dean gave a blessing, we heard once more the angelic voices of the St Martin's choir. And then we said our goodbyes and went our separate ways.

I had been asked by a few people over the course of that weekend how I'd become interested in pilgrimage. I explained that I first came to Canterbury in 1988 to be part of L'Arche, a wonderful world-wide organization where people with and without learning disabilities live, work and share life together. One of the highlights of the year for me was the pilgrimage. Each year in May or June the normal routine of life would be interrupted and people would walk together for four days. I relished that chance to journey with people along the North Kent coastline or through the countryside. Some years we even walked along the Pilgrims Way. As I've hinted at already, whether this was the actual route that any pilgrims to Canterbury would have taken is a moot point. It seems likely that pilgrims from London, and possibly other starting places too, would have come along Watling Street, the old Roman road. It was the quickest route and it would have been the best maintained. It would also have been the safest way. Medieval pilgrims had bandits as well as blisters to contend with, for those on pilgrimage would have had money with them and perhaps valuable gifts as well that would be left at the shrine at their journey's end. They would be seen as fair game by robbers. The government tried to assist by clearing trees alongside the road. These clearings were called tranches, after *tranche*, the French word for slice. In 1285 Edward I passed a law that made tranches compulsory. Major highways, of which Watling Street was perhaps the foremost, were to have a tranche of 200 feet on either side of wherever 'a man may lurk to do evil near the road.' It is said that these cleared areas can still be seen on each side of the current day A2 near Canterbury, between Harbledown and Boughton.

The pilgrimage from London, if taking that direct route, would have lasted about four days, just like our pilgrimage from St-Martin-in-the-Fields. It would have passed through Dartford, Rochester and Faversham and pilgrims would have made their overnight stops in one of the many hostels in these three towns.

Indeed Rochester gets a little mention in the Monk's Prologue of *The Canterbury Tales*. A couple of other places along the old Watling Street/A2 get a mention too, which would confirm the 'direct route' theory for those setting off from London. Sittingbourne is spoken of in the prologue to the Wife of Bath's Tale, and the prologue to the Yeoman's Tale makes mention of Boughton-under-Blean, which is between Faversham and Canterbury.

In my very first year at L'Arche I was asked to organise the pilgrimage. It would involve about fifty people setting off from Rochester and walking over five days to Canterbury, staying in church halls along the way. My fellow organiser was someone who was renowned as being rather a cantankerous character. However we sort of had fun driving around Kent visiting potential venues for fifty pilgrims to sleep and meeting people who would kindly offer meals as well as baths for those who needed them. We also struck some good deals at pubs who would do a buffet lunch for us.

My memory is very hazy now about the whole thing, although bedding down with fifty people on that first night in a church in Rochester made a lasting impression on me. A good night's sleep was out of the question due to the hard floor and the cacophony of snoring. Yet, there was also something wonderful about it. As several people on the St Martin's pilgrimage had remarked, the experience of walking, eating and sleeping together is a great leveller. And as I'd found myself, there's something very intimate about it. Also in common with the St Martin's pilgrimage I was so grateful for the kindness of those who were feeding us and accommodating us en route.

I remember nothing at all about our arrival at Canterbury Cathedral besides being pretty exhausted and looking forward to sleeping in my own bed again! As with any journey, the end of a pilgrimage can be something of an anti-climax, with the most significant experiences having happened on the way. That's why it's always advisable to not be in too much of a hurry to reach the destination and to have eyes and ears open to the little gifts and miracles that might be offered en route.

That was the last year that L'Arche Kent did a 'proper' sleep-out pilgrimage. Some people were getting too old for sleeping on the floor in a church hall and from 1990 we did a 'stay at home' pilgrimage which meant walking during the day, returning home to sleep and then re-starting the walk the next day. For a few years our route to Canterbury continued to overlap with the Pilgrims Way. Then one year in the early 2000s we decided to do something a bit different and came up with the idea of walking along the beautiful North Kent coastline. For many years thereafter, the L'Arche Kent annual pilgrimage started at Minster Abbey near Ramsgate with a time of prayer and singing with the enclosed Benedictine sisters and a fish and chip lunch. It then went along the coastline from Birchington, near Margate and passed by the old Roman fort at Reculver and took us through Herne Bay and on to Whitstable. The only thing that changed really, besides the people who were walking, was that the daily distances got shorter and shorter. What remained the same were the touching encounters that were had, the eating and praying together, the sharing of stories. Another fine tradition for me was a small intrepid group of us having a dip in the sea on the day we finished at Whitstable.

One year, a smaller group of us revived the old tradition of sleeping each night in church halls. We spent the final night in Whitstable and after our swim in the sea we sat and had a beer outside the Continental Hotel that overlooks the bay. I've often gone past that hotel when out cycling and I always remember with great fondness that time when a group of L'Arche pilgrims swam in the sea and had a beer at the Continental! Such are the simple pleasures of life on the road! One of those who swam and drank with me at the Continental is Liis, and her story is told below.

...PILGRIMS' TALES...
Pilgrimage - The place to Be

Before I joined a L'Arche Community, I had only read about pilgrimages in books and assumed that they went out of fashion centuries ago. Well I did grow up in Soviet Estonia, where religious roots were severed during the Second World War and trampled on during the following decades of occupation.

I loved my first L'Arche pilgrimage in the summer of 2000: walking from Meopham in London to Canterbury, being on the road for seven days and seven nights with a group of people with and without learning disabilities, sleeping in church halls and finally reaching the magnificent Canterbury Cathedral for a special service. I have been a pilgrimage convert ever since! Amongst other things, pilgrimages are an endless treasure trove of stories. So much happens and gets noticed when one is on a journey out of the ordinary.

One of my favourite L'Arche Kent pilgrimages was in May 2017. By then the walk was four days and sleeping in church halls a distant memory as most of us had grown to prefer the comfort of our own bed. In all other aspects pilgrimage was intact. There was a group of us together on a journey of spiritual exploration, exposed to the forces of nature, open in varying degrees to the possibilities of being lost.

My daughter was eight and on a school holiday. She had no choice but to join the pilgrimage. She was not best pleased as it meant having to get up in the mornings as if she was going to school, and a lot of walking. On top of that none of the other L'Arche kids were joining.

As our group of varied abilities started to walk through Blean woods in the dappled sunshine of late May something changed. With every step, the subdued and easily irritable child seemed to become lighter and happier. Soon no distance seemed too far and she was open to all experiences and encounters. I was delighted but baffled because as a family we had done many walks but none of them had had this sort of transformational effect.

Over the following three days more L'Arche kids joined. Somehow the word spread that pilgrimage was the place to be: way better than trampolining centres, roller skating arenas or highly organised play dates. As we walked there was a dizzying sense of freedom, adventure and unexpectedness, so much lacking from children's everyday highly regulated reality. Come to think of it, very much lacking from the lives of most adults too! With every step the world became a better place. The world of course had not changed at all, but our sense of belonging to it definitely had.

From then on (with a short break during the pandemic) all L'Arche Kent pilgrimages take place at May half-term, so that the youngest community members can also walk the world a better place.

Liis, Estonia

In gratitude for many years of L'Arche pilgrimages I wrote 'Pilgrimage Song.' The words are in English and French and I use the song each June when helping on a walking retreat in the French Alps for new L'Arche assistants.

Pilgrimage Song

We're walking, we're singing
As a pilgrim people we're bringing
Our need of each other, as a gift for the world

We're dancing and praying
In our welcome of difference we're saying
That each one is loved, and a gift for the world

Side by side, the fast and the slow
The old and the young, together we'll go
Telling our stories along the way
Sharing life together in the everyday

Nous marchons, nous chantons
Comme des pèlerins nous portons
Notre besoin des autres, comme un don pour le monde

Nous dansons, nous prions
Par nos différences nous disons
Que chacun est aimé, est un don pour le monde

Côte à côte, les rapides et les lents
Les vieux et les jeunes, nous marchons ensemble
Disant nos histoires sur le chemin
On partage notre vie dans le quotidien

The route of the L'Arche Kent pilgrimage has changed yet again but it still finishes at Canterbury, though not necessarily at the Cathedral. Some years we ended with a big celebration at the church of St Dunstan, which I pass every time I walk or cycle into the centre of the city. This beautiful old church has a significant place in the history of pilgrimage to Canterbury.

It was at St Dunstan's church that King Henry II arrived in 1174, having travelled by horse from London. Four years had passed since the brutal murder of Thomas Becket in the Cathedral, apparently under orders from the king. Henry had been a great reformer and had initially been aided in this work by Becket, who was his Lord Chancellor from 1155-1162 and Archbishop of Canterbury from 1162 until his death. However, the two later quarrelled over various issues, with Becket robustly defending the rights of the Church against encroachment by the Crown. The King was annoyed as well by Becket's propensity to excommunicate people i.e. banish them from the Church. The consequence for Becket was almost six years of exile in France.

Eventually there was a sort of reconciliation between the two in Normandy but Becket's subsequent return to England on December 1st 1170 stirred up further trouble. People were lining the streets of Canterbury to welcome him back to a Cathedral which had been decorated for the occasion; he refused to revoke his excommunications of several bishops; and he continued to speak out against the King. Things came to a head on Christmas Day with Becket foretelling his congregation in the Cathedral that he was about to be martyred, before proceeding to dish out a few more excommunications! The King had had enough and is said to have uttered the fateful words, "Will no one rid me of this turbulent priest?" This was heard by four knights who promptly made haste to Canterbury. They pursued Becket into the Cathedral, probably intending to arrest him. Becket resisted them, tensions rose and swords were drawn. Late in the afternoon of December 29th and near the High Altar, Becket was struck down with a fatal sword blow to the head. He was buried the next day in the crypt by his monks.

Four years later when Henry arrived at St Dunstan's Church, he changed into a rough woollen shirt and walked barefoot down St Dunstans Street to the Cathedral. As he knelt at the tomb of his erstwhile friend and Archbishop, he allowed himself to be hit five times by every bishop and canon present and three times by each of the monks! It was the final atonement for his part in the death of Thomas, and it marked out Canterbury as a major place of pilgrimage. It also gave rise to Geoffrey Chaucer's famous book about the kind of people who took part. Prior to this, poets had written in Italian and Latin, with English regarded as being rather a base and vulgar language by comparison. *The Canterbury Tales* was the first book of poetry to be written in English and so besides giving a fascinating and humorous insight into the adventures of medieval pilgrims it was of huge significance in the development of English literature.

The veneration of Thomas Becket began almost straight away, with the first organised pilgrimage in the summer of 1173, a few months after he had been canonised by Pope Alexander III. Following the rebuilding of the cathedral in the wake of the fire of 1174, Becket's body was removed from the crypt and re-interred in 1220 in a shrine in the new Trinity Chapel behind the High Altar. As with pilgrimage sites everywhere, the shrine was believed to be a place where miraculous events could occur. The stained glass in the Trinity Chapel depicts some of the miracles which are said to have taken place thanks to the intercession of St Thomas. These include a man being rescued after being buried alive and a drowned boy being brought back to life.

Also in common with pilgrimage sites the world over, having the relics of a saint or martyr could dramatically transform the fortunes of a town. For nearly four hundred years Canterbury prospered in the wake of the many pilgrims from all over Europe and even further afield who came and in the lavish gifts that they brought with them. Pilgrimages took place not just in the summer. Pilgrims came also in Lent, on the Feast of the Translation (or re-interment of the body) and on the anniversary of Thomas' death.

Regardless of where pilgrims had started their journey or what precise route they had taken, all would pass St Dunstan's church and make the final approach to the Cathedral along that same stretch that Henry had walked in his bare feet, and which I have walked or cycled along hundreds of times.

In 1220, the year of the re-interment of the body of Becket, and fifty years after his death, there began the practice of the Great Pardon or Jubilee. A pilgrim who made the pilgrimage in a jubilee year, which occurred every fifty years, would attain a plenary indulgence. This meant that all of a person's worldly sins were forgiven and they would go directly to heaven after their death, instead of having to spend time in purgatory, a sort of half-way house. The pilgrimage routes to Canterbury would be thronged each time there was a Jubilee. Sadly, the practice of indulgence was open to abuse. A wealthy person might send their servants off on pilgrimage on their behalf and claim the indulgence for themself. Or they might simply pay money for the indulgence!

The final Jubilee was in 1520 because in 1538, Henry VIII ordered Becket's shrine to be looted and for the bones to be burnt. Veneration of holy relics was banned, as was the practice of pilgrimage itself.

In those intervening four centuries, Canterbury had thrived and a whole hospitality industry had grown up to cater for the pilgrims. At one time, the city had one of the highest concentrations of pubs in England. And the reason for the many pubs and hotels just outside the city walls is that if pilgrims arrived too late in the day, the Westgate would be closed and they would have to find somewhere to spend the night, before completing their pilgrimage the next morning.

Howard Loxton remarks in his book *Pilgrimage to Canterbury* that

Canterbury Cathedral today 'sells no indulgences, only post-cards, guidebooks and souvenirs.' He points out as well that although there is no actual shine of St Thomas to see, the visitors to the Cathedral come now not in their thousands but in their millions. He wonders as well if those coachloads of tourists have more in common with Chaucer's motley band than with those who came in a spirit of penitence. 'They perhaps emerge with as great a sense of wonder,' he suggests, before going on to conclude, 'Thomas is not forgotten. Whatever happened to his bones, today his face and name are out there in every other shop in Canterbury.'

I'm happy as well to say that more than eight centuries after the murder of Thomas, pilgrimage on foot to Canterbury is alive and well, even if the original route may be in question. And, as can be seen from some of the stories in this chapter, it is still transforming the lives of those who take part.

CHAPTER 5

ROME

Outside Canterbury Cathedral there is a small stone tablet with the picture of a wide-brim-hatted pilgrim who looks like St James and the words 'Via Francigena.' This marks the beginning of the 1,700-kilometre-long pilgrimage route to Rome.

Occasionally when I attend evensong in the cathedral there is an announcement that someone is setting off for Rome in the morning. One such was Dustin in October 2022 and I was keen to speak with him about his motivation. He explained simply that he had done the Camino and was ready now for something longer! He certainly had something of the eternal traveller about him and he was clearly in good shape physically because he planned to take seventy-four days for his pilgrimage and to be in Rome on Christmas Eve, where he had requested a papal audience.

Phil McCarthy had been working as a doctor in Bristol when he stood by that stone tablet on the morning of March 24th 2008. Like Dustin he had received a blessing in the cathedral from one of the canons and his plan was to be in Rome in time for the feast of St Peter and St Paul on June 29th. Although rather slower than Dustin's schedule, it still meant having to cover fifteen miles a day, six days a week, with one rest day per week. It would take him in a straight line down through the length of France, and across Switzerland, skirting Lake Geneva. He would cross into Italy over the Alps at the Great Saint Bernard Pass and later climb the Apennines towards the Mediterranean before continuing South through Tuscany. As with pilgrims on the Camino, he had with him his pilgrim passport which would be stamped en route. He also had a long list of possible accommodation and a collection of maps. These, he was to discover, would be of limited use!

It was Phil's fiftieth year and his twentieth as a partner in his GP practice and he was in need of a break. At the start of his book *Rome Alone* he writes of his hopes for the walk: "A physical and a psychological challenge, a break from my responsibilities and an opportunity to live in the moment, to be open to unconventional encounters and to be more closely in touch with the planet." He also relished the chance to have time and space to be silent and to reflect and, in addition, he was raising money for two charities close to his heart.

The route of the Via Francigena had first been written down in AD 990 by a clerk in the party of Archbishop Sigeric. Like all Archbishops of Canterbury he had to go to Rome to receive from the pope his pallium or sign of office. The Via Francigena thereafter became the accepted route of English pilgrims travelling to the Eternal City and it even continued South from Rome for those wanting to carry on to Jerusalem. The way fell into disuse from the time of the Reformation until it was rediscovered and re-opened in the 1990s. That didn't mean that the route was easy to follow, as Phil was to find out. Especially in Italy, the Via Francigena signposts could be misleading or simply non-existent.

Apart from unhelpful or stolen signposts, Phil was to experience many others of the perennial pitfalls awaiting pilgrims. He got hopelessly lost on several occasions; he had excruciating pain in his feet, caused partly by having bought cheap boots (this was alleviated by the purchase of a better pair, as well as taking extra rest days); and he was bitten by a variety of dogs. For this latter problem he was grateful to be given by a fellow-pilgrim in Italy a device which made a high-pitched noise unpleasant to canines! A further irritant in Italy was being jeered at by local young men in bars. Or at least, that was Phil's perception on those days when he was feeling particularly sensitive and vulnerable. His solution to that issue: he realised that he could do nothing about the attitudes of others but could alter his own, and he resolved to 'stay calm!'

Phil's journey hadn't got off to the best of starts. There were flurries of snow as he walked out of Canterbury on that first early-spring morning and it was cold and grey; so too when he got off the ferry in Calais. France looked vast, his adventure seemed foolhardy and he doubted his ability to get to the end. Just like on my first day walking from Porto in the heat, Phil asked himself why he was doing it and whether there could possibly be anything spiritual about the whole crazy business.

And yet, in spite of the blisters and the bites, and the getting lost, and getting soaked, and the frustrations, and even the fury about having his bank card swallowed one day by a cash machine, he was often on the receiving end of small acts of kindness. At the end of his stay in a rather dismal hotel in one town the owner refused payment for dinner or drinks once he heard about the walk. He also presented Phil with some pâté for lunch. Phil was equally grateful for the warm hospitality he received in a succession of convents, monasteries, priest houses and private dwellings. On more than one occasion he was entrusted with the keys to the house and payment for the accommodation was refused. On other occasions his heart melted when smiled at by attractive young women…or attractive older women! And he concluded at one point, "As so often after a bad experience a good one followed."

Phil became more attentive to the natural world. He noticed the wildflowers, so too the insect burrows on the old log where he sat one day to eat his lunch. On some such days he had a feeling of elation and he reflected that "Every day was bringing new places, people and experiences. I was free of responsibilities and living more spontaneously." He noted a little later that, "Even the sheep and cows seemed friendly!"

There was pleasure to be had in eating a simple lunch on a bench in a beautiful place. He wrote of one such alfresco meal in Italy: "Soft local bread, sweet, slightly sweaty cheese and pears. It was wonderful: the food, the view, the breeze, warm sun and shade." That mirrored an experience I had when visiting a communist-era Prague in 1989. I'd gone into a shop which sold just one kind of bread and one kind of cheese and I was lucky that day that they also had tomatoes. I sat on a bench and bit into that bread which was made of rye and had little caraway seeds and it was delicious, so too the cheese. And the tomatoes were the tastiest and juiciest

I'd ever had. Bread, cheese and tomatoes eaten in an interesting place: it was an absolute feast.

Phil met scarcely any other pilgrims as he made his way down through France. He got used to his own company and it gave him space to think and reflect. He was happy, though, to cross paths with a variety of characters in Italy, especially two vivacious Italian women Barbi and Manu, with whom he shared several meals and interesting conversations. The three had a memorable day walking up and over the Cisa Pass into Tuscany. Phil was still spotting wildflowers and he was having fun asking Manu for the names in Italian.

Phil was excited to see the first signs to Rome, as the distance to his destination becomes shorter and shorter. He finally made it to the Tiber and onwards into the city on June 25th, three months and a day after setting out from Canterbury. As he walked past the palm trees on the Via della Conciliazione and into St Peter's Square and saw the enormous basilica bathed in early evening sunshine his mood was "calm and peaceful." And he was overjoyed to see standing by the obelisk, as agreed, his beloved wife Cath.

Over a meal at the curiously named 'Seven Deadly Sins' restaurant, Cath asked her husband if he had achieved his aims for the walk. He had certainly profited from the long break, he had raised £4,000 for his two charities, he had found time to reflect. And on the subject of getting fitter, he had lost ten kilograms, reduced his cholesterol, lowered his blood pressure, and he was able subsequently to run the Bristol Half Marathon twenty minutes faster! As if these were not impressive outcomes in themselves, he articulated years later many other benefits that are perhaps less tangible but no less significant.

...PILGRIMS' TALES...

Is this a Pilgrimage?

I was often asked, "Is this a pilgrimage?" Unsure what pilgrimage means in our age, and reluctant to be pigeonholed into piety, I obfuscated. Three months later I arrived in Rome and was delighted to be welcomed as a pilgrim in St Peter's Basilica. I had been changed by the journey. Over the years since, I have become convinced that walking pilgrimage is a countercultural sign pointing us towards the Common Good.

The personal benefits of long-distance walking are great and walking pilgrimage is increasingly seen as a contribution to developing small scale sustainable tourism. In my view the most important impact of pilgrimage is its witness to a better way.

Anyone who reads *The Canterbury Tales* will know that pilgrimage and tourism, trade and travel, and the sacred and profane have long been intertwined. Tourism in the West is a multi-billion-pound industry bringing consumers and providers together often in impersonal and sometimes dehumanising ways. In contrast a walking pilgrim is marginal to, or even outside of, this transactional market. Where the tradition of pilgrimage is alive, those who provide hospitality share in the journey, sometimes in deeply personal ways. I vividly remember a woman who ran a pilgrim hostel in Italy who insisted on washing and kissing the feet of her guests. This was a challenge to my English sensibilities, but there was no doubt of her welcome! Pilgrim accommodation can be basic and is sometimes gratuitous. In one parish when I asked about donating in return for food and accommodation, the parish priest said, "Here is the pilgrim box. If you have money, you can put some in; if you have no money then don't worry. But if you need money, take some out."

A pilgrim is on a covenantal journey along a path that generations may have trod in the past, and she or he walks it in the hope that future generations will follow. There is a defined route and a clear destination: pilgrimage is not wandering at whim. Pilgrimage is a counter to the widespread worship of individualism which undermines the Common Good. The experience of pilgrimage is not of autonomy but of vulnerability to the elements and of dependence on the kindness of strangers. The slowness of a journey in direct contact with the earth is a humbling reminder that we are fragile and transient embodied beings. Walking pilgrimage challenges the shallow rootlessness of our hyper-mobile society because it is an act of remembering, reenacting and reliving a deep tradition.

Pilgrimage counters the fear of the stranger, the marginalisation and demonisation of the other. It often leads to encounters which enable deep conversations with those from radically different backgrounds and world views. Such personal interactions are building blocks of the Common Good and an antidote to the polarisation of our society.

The tourist industry often promotes an 'exclusive experience.' In contrast, staying in a pilgrim hostel is an inclusive experience; you have no idea who will be sleeping in the next bunk. Pilgrims tend to use public or shared transport to the start and finish of their pilgrimage, and walking uses public spaces with no entry fees or tickets. Whilst a tourist looks for authenticity in the absence of other tourists, for the pilgrim the presence of other pilgrims at the shrine or on the path confirms its authenticity.

Today walking pilgrimage is a sign of hope and of true freedom. A pilgrim is not seeking to escape the world. Even without being fully aware of it, she or he is engaging profoundly with the world and responding to the call to become holy: wholly human, in communion with others, with creation and with the transcendent reality of God. That is the ultimate Common Good. Whether we walk long distances or not, we can all respond to that call as we make our journeys through our brief and often difficult lives.

Phil, England

Phil had with him on his walk to Rome a copy of a book called *In Search of a Way*. It was written by Gerry Hughes, a Jesuit priest who spent ten weeks in the summer of 1975 walking from Weybridge, near London, to Rome. The previous year he had made an eight-day retreat on a remote Scottish island called Eileach an Naoimh, meaning 'the rocky islet of the saints' and which had been home to both St Brendan and St Columba. As he sank into the silence of that place he described how "The beauty and the peace of that isle began to take hold of me, still me, teach me. It was like an inner cleansing of the mind and senses." He also began to notice simple things as if for the first time: the rocks, the wildflowers, the gulls. He had a sense of being at one with the world around him and he came to the realisation that "Life is a gift." Hughes described thus the motivation for his pilgrimage: "I decided to walk to Rome, not only because I wanted to study there and have always liked walking but because I wanted to recapture and deepen the island experience." He pointed out as well that the first thing that St Ignatius, the founder of the Jesuit order, did following his 'Damascus-like' conversion was to go on pilgrimage. In 1522, he walked the 340 miles from his family's home in Loyola in the Basque country to Manresa, near Barcelona. Then in 1523, he walked to Rome. He also insisted that all Jesuit novices should go on pilgrimage for a month, with little or no money. This is along that route that Ignatius himself followed and which is known as the Camino Ignaciano. It was the route taken in 2022, 500 years after Ignatius, by Jimmy from Dublin who I met on the way to Santiago and who told me his incredible story, as related in Chapter Three.

Gerry Hughes described *In Search of a Way* as being about 'two journeys', the first being the physical act of the walk, the second a spiritual quest. He said he set out on the former in order to find direction in the latter. He had some interesting insights on the way. One was the basic observation that in some towns and villages the people were kind and welcoming whereas in some places the people seemed unfriendly and unhelpful. He realised that when he was himself feeling upbeat and pain-free the people were kind and welcoming. On the other hand, on those days when he was feeling morose and had aching feet then the people were unfriendly! This appears to mirror the experience of Phil McCarthy. On the days in Italy when he wasn't feeling great, he had the impression that the young men in the bars were jeering at him! Hughes concluded that "the real obstacle on our journey to God is not heat, thirst, blisters, roadblocks, or other people, but the inner workings of our own minds, our inherited and unquestioned ways of perceiving ourselves and the reality around us."

In common with Phil's experience, Gerry became more sensitive to the reactions of those he encountered and he was elated by simple acts of kindness. He was overjoyed at the end of a long day's walk to be allowed to camp in somebody's field and to be brought a cup of coffee by the woman of the house. He remarked, "I have rarely enjoyed a cup of coffee so much." Also in common with Phil, he delighted in the natural world, especially the mountains, and noted that "After a day in their presence something of their stillness seeps into the soul." It would seem that he had indeed recaptured and deepened the experience of being on retreat on that remote Hebridean island of Eileach an Naoimh.

Not everyone has the time or the ability to walk to Rome in one go. Just like with the Camino, some people do it in stages. One such is Fr John Deehan who began in 2013 to walk sections of the Via Francigena with a group of fellow priests from the Archdiocese of Westminster in London. Their starting point was the Great Saint Bernard Pass in Switzerland, just before the Italian border. They spent a few days each year working their way down through Italy, except during the COVID outbreak when travel was impossible. In 2022 they resumed their walk from Bolsena in Lazio, the scene of the eucharistic miracle that hastened the adoption of the Feast of Corpus Christi throughout the Latin Church. From Bolsena they walked for forty-five miles over three and a half days and reached Viterbo, with Rome almost in sight.

They needed one final trip to reach the end point of the journey, the tomb of St Peter.

This has been a pilgrimage destination now for almost two millennia. The practice became popular from the fourth century with the Edict of Milan in 313, which gave freedom of worship to all religions including Christianity. In the decades to follow, a church was built over the site of Peter's martyrdom and burial, and this stood until the 16th century when Julius II commissioned the new Basilica of St Peters to be built. Meanwhile, the first church on the site of St Paul's burial was consecrated by Pope Sylvester in the 4th century, with the current Basilica of St Paul Outside the Walls being reconstructed in the 19th century. Pope Damasus (366-384) ensured that the catacombs were given proper care and he had them decorated with pieces of scripture. These acted as signposts for pilgrims from the fourth to the eighth centuries. In about 365, St Jerome recalled childhood memories of large crowds of pilgrims visiting the catacombs and the martyr churches in Rome. The feasts of the martyrs would have seen particular influxes of visitors into the city. Due to the close association with Peter and Paul, pilgrimage to Rome became known as *ad limina apostolorum*, to the threshold of the apostles.

In those first centuries, pilgrims benefited from the well-maintained system of Roman roads. That was until barbarian invasions and the breakup of the Roman empire made pilgrimage a perilous activity. Many people began instead to travel to Santiago.

The practice of pilgrimage to Rome was revived when Pope Boniface VIII declared 1300 a Jubilee (Holy) Year. Huge numbers of people arrived in the city, drawn by the promise of a plenary indulgence. This was the case again in 1350. Up to a million people flocked to Rome after Pope Clement VI declared that anyone who visited the martyr churches would be granted a plenary indulgence and therefore a remission of all earthly sins. However, the practice was abused as it had been elsewhere. The sins to be forgiven might be those of a wealthy patron for whom a pilgrim was walking as a proxy. Alternatively, people could simply pay to receive their indulgence rather than having to walk for days or weeks. This not only led to the Church getting a bad name; it also led to fewer people going on pilgrimage.

The Jubilee Years of 1450 and 1500 saw further large influxes of pilgrims coming to Rome but the practice of pilgrimage effectively ended with the Protestant Reformation which began in 1517 with Martin Luther. The sale of indulgences had been a particular bone of contention for the German reformer.

In spite of the Reformation, plus wars and instability in Europe in the following centuries, the practice of pilgrimage to Rome began again gradually. At the start of the 20th century, numbers of visitors to the Eternal City soared with the advent of mass public transportation. In the Jubilee year of 2000, there were 25 million pilgrims who visited the city, only a tiny proportion of whom would have walked any distance at all to reach the tomb of St Peter.

For John Deehan, pilgrimage is a time of renewal and a chance to do something a bit out of the ordinary. He considers it to be different to a holiday and, in a similar vein to Gerry Hughes, more akin to a retreat. He sees a geographical goal but also a personal goal. Part of the latter for him is walking over distances and terrains that he wouldn't do in the normal course of life. The pilgrimage also brings him up against his limits. He mentions that on one especially tough uphill stretch he dreamed of a taxi drawing up alongside and driving him to that night's destination. I assured him that pilgrims through the ages would have experienced similar fantasies! An important feature of the pilgrimage for John and his priest colleagues are the spiritual talks they receive on the way, reminding them that the pilgrimage for them is a symbol of the following of Christ and the renewal of their vocation as priests and servants of the Church.

Ian and Alison are a married couple that were partway through their second walk to Rome when I met them and I was fascinated to hear their story. Alison had taken part in her first Student Cross pilgrimage to Walsingham in 1976 when she was a student at Warwick. This annual event is now called Pilgrim Cross and more is written of that in Chapter 8. Alison met Ian in 1982 at a ball in Brighton and in terms of long-distance walking they've barely paused for breath!

In 2010, they had walked from Walsingham to Portsmouth, caught a ferry to Le Havre, then a bus to Honfleur, and from there they walked all the way to Vézelay, a defensible old hill town about midway between Paris and Lyon. Ian and Alison had been informed by friends that Vézelay was the starting point for one of the ancient Camino routes to Santiago. Other French routes begin at Paris, Le Puy and Arles. They kept going after Vézelay and their 2010 pilgrimage, which had begun in Walsingham on April 4th, Easter Sunday, ended in Santiago on July 19th after 101 days of walking. Plus a few rest days!

2010 was significant in that it was a Holy Year in Santiago, a practice which had started in 1122. These are years when the feast of St James, July 25th, falls on a Sunday. Pope Calixtus had declared that in such a year anyone who visited the shrine of St James would be granted a plenary indulgence. Usually in a Holy Year there would be a large increase in the number of pilgrims who are allowed to enter the cathedral in Santiago through the 'Holy Door', which is opened only in such years. Due to COVID there was no such influx of pilgrims in the next Holy Year of 2021. As a result, it was extended to the whole of 2022 which helped to ensure that the tradition remains popular, and with the next Holy Years due in 2027, 2032, 2038 and 2049.

The couple had set off for Santiago again in 2012, although this time their pilgrimage was in stages. They continued in 2013 and recall meeting a woman from Melbourne in an *albergue* in Villamayor de Montjardin who knew somebody that Alison worked with. *El mundo es un pañuelo!* The world is a handkerchief. Had she been from Newry I'm sure she would have known someone who knew my Uncle Pat!

In 2014, they walked from Oviedo to Melide on the Camino Primitivo. This is so called because, as Jimmy explained to us all on that memorable boat trip to Padrón, it was the first Camino to be established when in 814, King Alfonso II of Asturias walked from Oviedo to Santiago, then known as Mount Libredón. Ian and Alison had to cut short their pilgrimage at that point as Alison's father was ill and died a few months later. They came back in 2015 and walked from Ferrol to Santiago on the Camino Inglés. That route gets its name by being the one that would have been taken by many pilgrims coming from Britain, as well as Ireland and elsewhere in Northern Europe. They would have come by boat to the ports of A Coruña or Ferrol and walked from there. From Santiago, Ian and Alison went on to Finisterre. In 2019, they finally continued on the Camino Francés, which they'd set off on in 2012, when they walked from León to Sarria.

A particular spiritual highlight for Alison on the Camino Francés was at the promontory between the mountains at La Faba, on the way to O Cebreiro. For her this was one of those 'thin places' i.e. a place where one can almost reach out and touch heaven. I had a similar sense at that very place, so too at Castrojeriz, a town at an elevation of over 800 metres and commanding vast views in every direction. I have had this sense as well at the top of Glastonbury Tor, even from its more modest height of 158 metres. It was in the tiny chapel of the grounds of the La Faba hostel that Ian and Alison received a pilgrim blessing from Santi, a Franciscan monk. He also advised them that on arrival in Santiago they should go to the Franciscan convent behind the Cathedral. At 3 p.m. every day they open their small refuge for pilgrims for a blessing on a first come, first served basis. Ian and Alison followed Santi's advice and this was a fitting moment of completion for them on their first pilgrimage to Santiago.

In 2017, Ian and Alison had set out to walk to Rome. Having walked to Santiago and the (alleged) tomb of St James, the next logical step for them was to Rome and the tomb of St Peter. They had begun that particular pilgrimage from their home in Elephant and Castle in London, having obtained the first pilgrim stamp from St George's Cathedral. They walked to Newhaven, where they caught a ferry to Dieppe and then continued walking to Paris. From Paris they set off on the Camino route down through France to St-Jean-Pied-de-Port, the town where many people, myself included, have begun the Camino Francés to Santiago.

They wanted to visit the well-known Marian shrine of Lourdes en route and they remember how poignant it was to reach that place via the Pyrenees. "There's something unique about arriving by foot in a pilgrimage destination," Ian points out. "It's as if God had wanted me to get a good experience of Lourdes." He explains as well that because they came down into the town from the mountains they found themselves immediately at the Basilica and the grotto, rather than having to pass through the commercial centre like most pilgrims. They also had a special task to perform in the grotto. When they'd been in Paris they'd got talking to the owner of a Sports Bar who was a Coptic Christian. He was excited to hear that they were going to Lourdes and gave them five euros to light there a candle for each member of his family.

From Lourdes Ian and Alison walked across the South of France towards Carcassonne and the Mediterranean. All of the other pilgrims were walking in the opposite direction, towards St Jean and Santiago. The only pilgrim they met who was walking East like them was Malachy from Ireland who was on a summer break from Plum Village, the community in the South of France that was home to the Vietnamese monk, poet and peace campaigner, Thich Nhat Hanh. Malachy asked them why they were going the 'wrong' way! They duly explained.

Alison is adamant that, "Pilgrimage is not just a nice walk." For her, "It's getting to a destination and it's important to be visible." She adds that "It's a faith witness, an opportunity for prayer, and you need to be sociable with people." She also sees how those living along pilgrimage routes identify with all of that and are happy to help the passing pilgrims. She goes on: "It's about an intention to find God or to come closer to God on the journey or to find something at the destination." She also refers to the American peace activist, Jim Forest, a great friend of Thich Nhat Hanh, who urges us to "Make the whole of our life a pilgrimage."

Dawn Champion of the British Pilgrimage Trust, BPT, also considers pilgrimage to be about intention. She views it as a walk with a purpose, during which a person might be seeking to let go of something or to add something to their life, or perhaps wrestle with a question. For her the pilgrim sets out with the expectation of finishing their journey a different person: in short, transformed. Dawn noted as well the interesting finding of the BPT that 40% of people walking on pilgrimage routes describe themselves as Christian, a further 40% call themselves spiritual, and the remaining 20% neither. Regardless of the category, common motivations for walking are connecting with nature and connecting with oneself. It's also fascinating to observe that pilgrimage is the fastest growing form of travel in Europe, with 18–25-year-olds the largest demographic within that. In an age where people are leaving the Church in their droves there is clearly still a thirst for the kinds of experience that pilgrimage can provide: meaningful connections, an opportunity for self-exploration, and a chance to see other places and encounter different cultures.

From Carcassonne, Ian and Alison carried on to the French Riviera and at Menton crossed into Italy and joined the Via de la Costa. From there they were on the Via Francigena, upon which they had the strong feeling of walking in ancient footsteps, following as it does the old Roman roads. They remember with a smile staying for two nights in a place in Genoa and wondering why people were coming and going throughout the night. They discovered that they were in the red-light district! I can say from my own experience as well that you certainly end up in some interesting places when on pilgrimage, besides brushing up against some interesting characters!

On their eventual arrival in Rome after 149 days on the road they were met in St Peter's Square by a lady called Ann Farr who is a member of Pax Christi and who I have met myself through an Irish Chaplaincy retreat that I was leading. They said they got a bit lost coming into Rome and this seems to be a not uncommon experience of pilgrims walking into the Eternal City; so too an initial sense of anti-climax. Having said that, for Ian and Alison and for countless pilgrims it is the journey that is perhaps more important than the destination.

Their second pilgrimage to Rome began in July 2022 at St Patrick's Church in Waterloo in London. They walked to Canterbury along the Pilgrims Way and went to Evensong in the cathedral and saw other pilgrims to Canterbury that they had met on the path. The Via Francigena took them to Dover and the ferry to Calais. From there it was down through France and back over the Alps via the Great Saint Bernard Pass that Guy Stagg (mentioned in the next chapter) had traversed in the depths of winter, and Phil McCarthy on a cold and misty spring day. They stayed at the same monastery that Guy and Phil would have arrived at following their own herculean efforts. Built by Augustinian monks in the Middle Ages, it is called the Great Saint Bernard Hospice and is famed for its hospitality.

They continued on the Via Francigena through Italy and reached Sienna in October and there they were forced to stop. Since Brexit, UK passport holders can only stay in the EU for 90 days out of every 180 and they had reached their limit! They set off back to London on a meandering train journey, to allow for some "decompression time," as they put it. This took them through Florence, Milan and Paris and it was in the crypt of the cathedral in Milan that "a magical thing happened." They found themselves at the baptistry in the excavated crypt where Ambrose had baptised Augustine of Hippo at the Easter vigil of 387. Augustine subsequently adopted the Nicene, or more orthodox, practice which became the norm in the Christian Church. This contains the belief in a single, supreme God, as spoken of to this day in the Nicene Creed: 'I/we believe in one God...' Earlier in their pilgrimage, Ian and Alison had unexpectedly encountered St Augustine's Tomb in Pavia, so were pleased to make yet another connection on their travels, and one which was highly significant in the development of the Christian Church.

In answer to the question of why they keep walking, Ian and Alison say, "Because we can!" Ian adds that, "We thoroughly enjoy it," and for Alison it's "all about getting closer to God." They also stress how grateful they are for the experience and refer to a sense of "awe and wonder about the world." They mention the liminal nature of pilgrimage, whereby they step out of normal life and into a different space. This moving away from one's usual day to day life for a period of time mirrors my own experience and it appears to be a common factor for pilgrims everywhere.

"It strips everything back," they go on, "just putting one foot in front of the other. It's like being on retreat. Our day's work is walking from here to there." And their final words: "Aren't we lucky!"

I've been in Rome myself on two occasions. I'm afraid to say that both times I flew there and was more tourist than pilgrim but, as has been said already in this book, the two have been closely intertwined ever since pilgrimage began.

On the most recent visit, Yim Soon and I were happy to be staying in a sort of pilgrim hotel that was named after Our Lady of Lourdes and I was rather excited to be served breakfast by a nun! We set off on the first morning for St Paul's Outside the Walls, which is an enormous Basilica and, as the name suggests, outside of the original city boundary. Founded by the Emperor Constantine, the first Basilica was consecrated in 324, then enlarged and enhanced by later emperors and popes. We arrived, by chance, just in time for Mass, which was a quiet and prayerful affair and attended by just a handful of people. Following a fleeting visit to the tomb of St Paul we were off on a bit of a tourist trail. That, after all, is what most visitors to Rome do, pilgrims or otherwise.

In the evening we were unashamedly tourists, enjoying Happy Hour cocktails on one of the narrow streets near the Trevi fountain before strolling over to the Piazza Navona for a pizza and some very eclectic street entertainment. Firstly we were treated to 'Roma tap dance,' which was a woman in her 60s who would sing Adele's 'Someone like you' and follow it up with a little tap dance. She was followed by a man who must have been in his 70s and was, rather incongruously, wearing a T-shirt of a bearded John Lennon. He set up shop with his speaker on the pavement and launched into a set that went seamlessly from Pavarotti to Leonard Cohen and reached its climax with 'Volare.' I turned to the young English couple on the next table and remarked, "Rome's gypsy king!"

Even if it was a bit wacky it was a wonderful evening: enjoying food and drink and music in a city whose streets are suffused with history, both sacred and secular, whilst connecting with interesting people. In essence, it wasn't too dissimilar to many of the evenings I'd spent on the Camino.

The next day we walked after breakfast (served again by aforementioned nun!) down the Spanish Steps and along the Via dei Condotti and then the Via Tomacelli, over the Tiber and past the Castel Sant'Angelo and finally down the Via della Conciliazione and into St Peter's Square. As with the previous day, we arrived by chance just in time for Mass. Unlike at St Paul's Outside the Walls this service was packed with people. There were pilgrims/tourists from all over the world and readings were in several languages. I'm not always a great fan of big solemn Masses in grand venues but I was touched on this occasion. I'm not sure why exactly; perhaps the sense of being part of a tradition that is so universal and so long-lasting. It was certainly one of the highlights of my second Roman holiday!

Another person who, like me, found himself in Rome part tourist/part pilgrim was a friend, fellow-musician and bard, and the final words of this chapter go to him.

…PILGRIMS' TALES…
Roma: Odi et Amo

Catullus, the ancient Roman poet, wrote 'Odi et Amo' (I hate and I love) about a certain paramour. I feel the same way about his city, La Bella Roma.

I was a curious hybrid, half tourist/half pilgrim, on arrival in the Eternal City. It was twilight when I got my walking shoes and suddenly found myself standing on Capitol Hill. Wow! Here I am, in the footsteps of the Caesars, under Romulus & Remus, looking down on the ruins of the Roman Forum. I'd studied Latin at school, Classics in College, but nothing had prepared me for this. I was standing on history, geography, language, and the destiny of the early Christian martyrs. Compared to the constant noise of its modern metropolis the atmospheric silence of the Roman Forum in ghostly twilight was otherworldly.

And it isn't called The Eternal City for nothing. Not following a rigid grid system like many other cities, it seems to follow the sinuous curves of the River Tiber. So, if you walk long enough around Rome you'll probably end up where you began. I wandered round and round with my map to try and find the place called the 'Vicolo di Ripa' where an old Blues legend was playing a gig. I eventually located him in a basement bar, as related in my song 'The Night I Nearly Played with Louisiana Red.' But that's another story.

On the negative front (Odi) I wasn't impressed with those people, Roman or otherwise, who harangued tourists, one way or another: the pickpockets who picked my father's pockets, not once but twice, near the Stazione Termini, the main train station. Thankfully all they got was a rusty comb and a handkerchief. Worse still though was the opportunistic taxi driver who took my parents on a long-winded tour of the very Eternal City, when all they wanted to do was get from A to a not very distant B. My parents had no words of Italian, the driver pretended he had no English, and he robbed them of most of their ruby anniversary holiday money. 'Cave Canem!' (Beware of the dog!). I say, 'Cave Cowboys!' Rome is full of them.

Thankfully the positive (Amo) far outweighed the negative aspects of Rome. My highlights were cultural and spiritual, had to do with the mind and the soul, and often in Rome I found it difficult to differentiate between the two. The artistic and the spiritual seemed to meld together as one. And, as Rome sits on seven hills, I give you in parting the seven reasons I hope to return to Rome.

7) FONTANA DI TREVI: Probably best known for Anita Ekberg's antics therein, in Fellini's film *La Dolce Vita*, the rumour goes that if you throw a coin into the fountain you will always return to Rome. Must have done so, as I've been there twice.

6) THE PANTHEON: This big old black blob of a building confronts you as you turn a corner in Rome. And when you wonder has it anything to offer, you see MARCUS AGRIPPA FECIT inscribed on the portico. In you go,

and, mindless of the architectural achievement of this ancient edifice, your eyes look upwards to the vast gaping hole in the roof which lets in all kinds of weather.

5) PIETA: Michelangelo's sculpture of Madonna cradling the body of Jesus, after the cross. One of the toughest men I ever met told me "Ho pianto," (I cried) after seeing it.

4) CIRCUS MAXIMUS: When Rome is too much, the traffic chaotic, even the incredible art and architecture overwhelming, there is only one place to go...to breathe...to get away from it all...a most unlikely spot...The Circus Maximus. Yes! The site of the old chariot races. It is a green oblong oasis in the middle of the mad city.

3) NEW TESTAMENT: Whenever I read the words "And so we came to Rome" in the Acts of the Apostles (28:14) they always hit to the heart. As a Christian, the significance of this city cannot fail to overwhelm me at times. Paul's letter to the Romans. St. Peter in chains. And the Colosseum: gateway to heaven for the early martyrs.

2) JOHN KEATS: Probably the first great poet I fell in love with, in my mid-teens. 'The Eve of St. Agnes' is unequalled. With my father I visited his house on the Spanish Steps, where he lived for a while, and died at the tender age of twenty-six. Alone I visited his grave, not far from the Arch of Constantine, adorned with a single red rose, eternally.

1) THE CATACOMBS: My Roman odyssey ends underground, in the catacomb of San Callisto. Some say morbid. I say, like I said about the Forum, otherworldly. The humming buzz of modern Rome is drowned out in the silent sanctuary of the catacomb. Yes, it is full of skulls and bones, an ancient burial site, but so much more besides. No pollution here...the air is supernaturally clear. The slightest sound is profound,

and the Eternal City has nothing more to offer than the portal to eternity itself.

Peter, Ireland

CHAPTER 6

JERUSALEM

Guy Stagg set out for Jerusalem from Canterbury on January 1st 2013. After attending the morning office of Matins in the Cathedral and receiving a blessing from the Dean in the Trinity Chapel (close to where the shrine to Thomas Becket had been) he began his journey of 5,500 kilometres on foot that would take ten months and bring him across ten countries. He had been through a difficult period in his life, which had included thoughts of suicide. "Departing from Canterbury," he wrote, "I thought I was leaving the world behind." Tough as it was to be walking long distances each day with a heavy rucksack and in the middle of the winter, he described the exhilaration he felt in journeying alone all the way down through France and, in particular, being the first pilgrim in decades to cross the Alps in the winter via the Great Saint Bernard's Pass.

Those that Guy encountered on the way had a variety of motivations for walking. Giacomo, an athletic looking man in his sixties who was staying at the same convent in Tuscany, was en route to Rome and covering long distances every day without any breaks. He declared that, "Pilgrimage is not a holiday." This is similar to the attitude of 'We are not here to make party' Hans who I met on the Camino. For many of those going on pilgrimage in the Middle Ages it was very much a holiday; a chance to have a break from the normal routine for a few days or weeks and to see some different places and meet some interesting characters. The majority of people at that time might spend their entire lives not travelling much further than their own village. Indeed, the word pilgrim comes from the Old French *pelegrin* which in turn is derived from the Latin *per agrum*, beyond the fields. This gave rise to the word *peregrinus*, which meant stranger but could originally have meant any traveller.

Just as it had been for me and many others when I was on the Camino for the first time, it was not just a chance to 'go beyond the fields,' it was absolutely a party! And that didn't detract at all from the deeply spiritual experience I had and it may even have enhanced it. I met a few people like Giacomo on the Camino; John from Holland, for example, 'Mr 2,000 miles.'

Guy explained that the motivation for his pilgrimage was "not penance, nor protest, nor a race to Rome," rather the hope that a ritual could heal him. He found comfort in reading the entries in the guest book of an apartment for pilgrims and by seeing that countless people had gone before him not knowing the reason for their journey and hoping that it might all make sense when they reached the end.

When Stagg finally reached Jerusalem, he had a sense of disappointment and of disillusion. He felt no hint of the sacred and doubted whether his life has been transformed in any way by his arrival in the Holy City. He noted that his "imagination had conjured up trumpets, banners, fireworks and parades." The stark reality for him was that "alone I could pretend my journey mattered. Here I was just another pilgrim." Yet, he came to realise that "looking back on the last ten months, it was not the solitude I remembered, but the charity of so many strangers." He encountered in Jerusalem a man called James who at the age of thirty-one had given up all his possessions and travelled the world as a pilgrim for the next twenty-two years. He spent his summers in the Old City and one morning shared his meagre rations with Guy, who observed, "A man with no money sharing his breakfast with a stranger." Guy wondered what hurt had impelled James to leave home and family and to travel the world but concluded, "his motives did not matter. In the end, the kindness was all that mattered."

Gerry Hughes was another who felt compelled to make a pilgrimage to Jerusalem, and the title of the first chapter of *Walk to Jerusalem* will be familiar to anyone who has indulged in any form of extreme physical activity: 'I walk because I must.' The 1975 walk of Hughes to Rome is captured in his earlier book *In Search of a Way*, which is mentioned already in this book and in which he shows how the physical or 'outer' journey can shed light on the 'inner' journey that each of us must undergo and which will end with our death. *Walk to Jerusalem* is similarly an exploration of the physical journey through several countries and the inner journey encapsulated by the subtitle of the book, *In Search of Peace*.

As with Guy Stagg, Hughes faced hardships and low points but was constantly touched by the kindness of strangers, just as he had been when walking to Rome. He noted, "Throughout the pilgrimage I was amazed at the spontaneous generosity of people to a stranger and they seemed to delight in it." In common with my own experience, he had many striking coincidences along the way. At the end of one long day's walking in Germany he was, as usual, looking for a bed for the night. There were two hotels in the town but one was fully booked, the other closed. He went into a bar and asked the barman about lodgings whilst ordering a pint of Guinness which he sat and sipped whilst making petitions to 'the Celtic saints!' A young man who had overheard his enquiries took him to the house of the local pastor. The pastor's wife answered the door, welcomed them both in and said she was glad to see them because she had invited two people for coffee and cake and neither had turned up. Hughes and his companion were treated to a huge plate of cream cakes with coffee and later he was driven 7 km by the pastor to accommodation and discovered the next day that the bill had already been paid. Unbeknownst to the others, the day of the coffee and cakes had been Gerry's birthday.

As well as such experiences, which I almost came to expect when on the Camino, I could relate strongly to Gerry's delighting in the natural world when, for example, he wrote, "As I walked, I began to recover what had become so clear to me on the Rome walk, a sense of wonder at nature and a feeling of at-one-ness with it."

Also in common with my own experience and with that of Guy Stagg, and I suspect with that of countless other pilgrims, coming to the endpoint was an anti-climax for Gerry. He wrote of his journeys to Rome and to Jerusalem: "On both pilgrimages, I found the moment of arrival at the final destination to be strangely flat, especially my arrival at the main bus station in Jerusalem." It brought him, however, to the realisation that "the object of the journey was not so that I could find God at the end of it," and he concluded that "God is on the journey all the time, not just at the end of it." "The point of the journey," he noted, "was to learn this truth rather than to reach a particular destination, however holy, and there is no end to the exploration."

Hughes had recalled as well that "there were moments on the road to Rome and on the road to Jerusalem when I experienced a momentary glimpse of our unity with all things." He had felt this already in the Scottish Highlands when preparing for his walk to Rome and there were similar moments on each pilgrimage when he felt, even if only for a split second, at one with the trees swaying at the roadside. He wrote of these moments, "It was as though I was experiencing my own soul as conterminous with the universe."

Yet another long-distance walker is Henk who I mentioned in Chapter 3. I met him on the road to Santiago and had been curious to hear about his six-month journey on foot from his native-Netherlands to Jerusalem.

...PILGRIMS' TALES...

How I got rid of my black bag on the way to Jerusalem

I'd always wanted to go to Jerusalem. I had already walked the Camino de Santiago three times, and I had walked to Rome. Walking to Jerusalem following parts of the Templar Trail was the third big pilgrimage in Europe. I would belong to a handful of people, or perhaps I'm the only one, that has walked all three.

Often on my adventures I add a random element: going barefoot, carrying an egg on a spoon, or maybe taking a monkey with me. I decided to walk to Jerusalem with no money, and before leaving home I handed over my wallet, credit cards and cash to my dad. I was very nervous.

Some days I ate nothing. Some days I ate only dry bread. There were blisters, and vitamin deficiency where the skin began falling off my hands. And there were infestations of ants in my tent. Slugs that slimed their way across the little food stash I had. I got lost many times. Walking along the Croatian coast during the heat wave in the summer months was horrible. But by reframing the situation, by always focusing on the gift hidden inside the setbacks or adversity, I managed to keep moving forward. Instead of being annoyed by the ants, I focused on how they were actually cleaning up the bread crumbs in my tent. Instead of focusing on how frustrated I was about walking in the wrong direction for an hour, I focused on the fact that everyone I would meet from now on I wouldn't have met if I hadn't gotten lost. If I didn't eat for a day, I focused on how I learnt more about my body and how it reacts and functions when it doesn't get food. Insights not many people know about their own body, and I also thought that one day this would make a good story. By finding the hidden blessing inside your problem, challenge, or pain you become unstoppable.

My walking journey passed through thirteen countries: The Netherlands, Belgium, France, Switzerland, Italy, Slovenia, Croatia, Montenegro, Albania, Greece, Turkey, Cyprus and Israel. Due to instability in other countries en route, the only option from Turkey was to take the ferry to Cyprus, walk across Cyprus, and then take a ferry to the North of Israel. However, a ferry costs money, something I didn't have. To make matters worse, when I got to the harbour, where my plan was to offer to work on a boat or do magic entertainment on the boat (one of my hobbies), it turned out the last ferry of the season had already left. I was stuck. Stranded. I began to worry, and thought my journey was over. But then I remembered that the only way I could do anything on this trip was by meeting other people. So I went back into the city. I began talking to as many people as I could. Connecting with them, telling them inspiring stories from my trip, doing magic, and always telling them about my challenge of how I was going to get to Cyprus. And before I knew it, several people had come together and bought me a cheap flight!

In Albania, I'd desperately needed a shower and to wash my clothes. I walked into a hotel/restaurant, explained about my journey to the waiter, and asked if he maybe had some hot water for me. He went away and when he returned he offered me lunch, and then snuck me into one of the hotel rooms so I could take a shower.

You don't need many skills to make a trip like this. You just begin walking and you slowly get stronger. You don't need to be an expert navigator: you can just use Google Maps. You don't need to be fearless: you just burn your boats, so you have no choice but to find a way. What you do need is the right mindset; being able to reframe an event from bad to good. You need a smile on your face which will help you connect with people. And if you focus on giving back instead of taking you can give back in the form of sharing stories, sharing your talents, and by forging a human connection.

Aside from the right mindset, what you really need is faith in humanity, the belief that people will help you when in need. At the beginning of my journey I didn't yet truly believe. And so I had a black bag hanging off the side of my backpack. Every time people gave me food, I'd put a percentage of that in that black bag. It was my food stash, a backup for a rainy day. For the day when people would stop helping me. And I was sure that day would come. However, over time this bag become smaller and smaller, until eventually I got rid of it. This was the moment I truly began to believe that the kindness of strangers is something you can reliably depend upon.

Henk, Holland

Jerusalem has, like Rome, long been a destination for pilgrims, with the practice of Christians making a pilgrimage to 'The City of Peace' beginning in the fourth century. Emperor Constantine had credited his victory at the Battle of Milvian Bridge in 312 to the Christian God. Following the Edict of Milan the following year, Christianity became the official religion of the Roman empire.

A few years later, the mother of Constantine, Helena travelled to Jerusalem in a quest to excavate the Holy Places. On the site said by Helena to be that of the crucifixion and resurrection, Constantine ordered the building of an enormous Basilica. That was followed by other building projects financed by similarly wealthy benefactors. The religious tourism that resulted led to the same kind of growth in business and prosperity that has been seen in pilgrimage sites the world over. And just as in other places of pilgrimage, possession of holy relics could transform the fortunes of a town. They could also lead to some very unholy behaviour, such as people from a neighbouring town trying to steal those relics! They might also change hands at exorbitant prices. The relics of St Stephen, for example, were purchased by the fifth century Roman emperor Theodosius II for a stash of gold coins and a large gold cross. For those pilgrims not endowed with such largesse, a whole range of 'lesser' relics could be acquired for a small fee!

The holy sites themselves have also been subject to the most unholy of squabbling. In 2008, Israeli police were called in to break up a brawl that had broken out between monks at one of Christendom's most sacred places. The Church of the Holy Sepulchre is believed to be the place where Jesus was buried, and a group of Armenian priests had been having a procession to mark the discovery in the fourth century of the cross thought to have been used for the crucifixion. The Greek Orthodox were unhappy that the procession was taking place without one of their number present. Two monks, one from each side, came to blows and were later taken away in handcuffs!

Pilgrimage to Jerusalem had, for a few centuries, been almost exclusively reserved for the wealthy as it involved long and costly sea journeys. This all changed in the eleventh century because of two events. Hungary became a Christian nation, with Stephen I opening up the country's borders to pilgrims in 1018. At around the same time, Byzantine armies conquered the Balkans and so there was now a land route to Jerusalem from Western Europe. The growth of Benedictine monasteries providing hospitality along the way was one further factor that led to a surge in a kind of religious mass tourism. As said previously, many of those travelling would be doing so in a spirit of penitence and with the desire for their earthly sins to be expiated.

The military pilgrimage also became popular at this time, with the First Crusade undertaken by Urban II in 1095. Crusaders were promised salvation if they conquered Jerusalem, which they did in 1099. Those who took part in that and subsequent Crusades underwent starvation and disease on those long journeys. Their reward: a place in the heavenly kingdom! This promise of salvation was the first known use of the plenary indulgences that came to be a source of such controversy in the Roman Catholic Church. From the Crusades there also came the practice of selling indulgences. Wealthy patrons who were unable to go on a pilgrimage themselves could make a donation towards the war effort, whilst gaining the same heavenly reward as the Crusaders!

Once Jerusalem fell again into the hands of the Moors and with the failure of subsequent Crusades, it was no longer possible for Christians to travel there. They would go on pilgrimage instead to places like Rome or Santiago.

Long before the Advent of Christianity, Jerusalem had been a place of pilgrimage for Jews. There were three annual pilgrimage festivals commanded in Deuteronomy 16:16. These were in spring for Passover, in Summer for Shavuot, and in the Autumn for Sukkot, and evidence suggests that these were observed in practice by at least some Jews. However, this appears to have stopped with the destruction of the second temple in 70 CE, nearly 2,000 years ago. Since then, pilgrimage has not really been a relevant Jewish concept. Nowadays, there are Jewish journeys that might be described sociologically, though not theologically, as pilgrimages, for example a visit to Auschwitz or Yad Vashem; or psychologically, such as saying prayers at the grave of a loved one or a trip to the town in Eastern Europe that a great grandparent might have come from. Cliff Cohen made the interesting observation to me that nobody knows the location of the burial place of Moses. I reflected that in the Christian tradition, such a significant place would instantly be turned into a pilgrimage destination!

Cliff spent seven months in Jerusalem in the 1970s as part of his rabbinic training. It was for him a "magical city" and a place of deep spirituality, carrying as it does the interlinking stories of three major world religions, lived out over millennia. He noted the capacity of places to absorb and radiate part of their story. This rang true for me, following my experience on the Camino. Following hundreds of years of pilgrims walking that same way, there was a sense for me that the very stones had somehow become sanctified. At the same time, I wondered if it might be a way of showing us that all of the stones that we walk upon are 'holy ground,' if only we have eyes to see and ears to hear.

Cliff told me of a group he joined up with on Christmas Eve who were making the ten or twelve mile walk from Jerusalem to Manger Square in Bethlehem. It was a group that was wonderfully diverse in terms of nationality and language and tradition. He was struck by the sense of companionship; the root of which word is the sharing of bread. There was a sharing of both food and stories on that walk and Cliff had an insight into what people gained from the experience of being on pilgrimage. He noted that people were sharing their faith with one another and that there was a sense of unity in the diversity. Some of those present decided to walk back the following day with those they had got to know on the way and with whom a profound bonding had taken place.

Religious experience is not to be found by chasing it, in Cliff's view, but by being open to it. Religion provides a doorway and we don't even need to know whether that doorway is open. He viewed pilgrimage in a similar light. It could be a catalyst for an inner process of transformation, and it might only be apparent much later what a life-changing event if had been. Cliff stressed that it can be helpful to take an extended period away from the usual day-to-day existence in order to move some of the clutter away from the aforementioned doorway. It is only when we allow ourselves to step away that we have the opportunity to see what may have been right in front of our noses. I mentioned to Cliff that that's just what those medieval pilgrims to Canterbury and other places were doing. They were taking a bit of time out from their everyday lives to meet some interesting characters, to see some picturesque countryside, and to view life from a different perspective. And whether the destination is Canterbury, Santiago, Rome, Jerusalem or wherever, that's surely what pilgrims have always been doing; and what they'll continue to do.

On his several visits to Jerusalem, Fr Anthony Charlton has been especially touched to be so close to some of those places related to the life of Christ and it breathes new life into those passages from the Bible that tell, for example, of Jesus' passion and death. He tells of how being there and going into certain ancient churches was like reading a fifth gospel. For him it is not just a case of visiting sites but of reliving the scriptures. "The scriptures come alive," he remarks. I hoped that this might be the case for me too on what was my very first visit to Jerusalem. I ended up getting a lot more than I bargained for.

Yim Soon and I flew to Israel in October 2023. We'd chosen that time of year in the expectation of temperatures that would be comfortably in the mid-twenties for our few days of walking pilgrimage prior to arriving in the Holy City. Our walk was to begin in Nazareth. What was a village of only about 100 dwellings when Jesus lived there is now a bustling city of nearly 80,000 and the largest Arab town in Israel. It's also the start of the 'Jesus Trail', which goes 65 km to the Sea of Galilee.

One of the first things I discovered about Nazareth is that you don't need an alarm clock there! If you hadn't already been woken up by the various cocks crowing, there was the Muslim call to prayer at 5.15 a.m., followed in turn by bells peeling at 6 a.m. from, presumably, one of the Christian churches. Or maybe more than one: they were making enough noise! I took that as my cue and left our guest house to have a wander just as dawn was breaking. Two men were walking with intent through the narrow streets of the Old City so I decided to follow them, figuring that they must be going somewhere! They were indeed going somewhere, to the huge Basilica of the Annunciation that we'd passed the evening before when trying to locate our lodgings.

It had been quite a journey from Tel Aviv, and quite a trip so far. As has been related so many times already in this book, pilgrimage is inevitably filled with encounter and with kindness. We'd had plenty of both before we'd even got onto the trail. And our one-night stay in Tel Aviv had truly been a little taste of paradise, which included swims in the warm Mediterranean and some great food. But then we had to get ourselves to Nazareth. We managed to find the right local bus, and a little later were at a very chaotic and sad looking Central Bus Station. The glamour of the beach seemed a world away already!

We eventually located the Nazareth bus that left at 4 p.m. for a supposed 2 ½ hour journey. Due to endless traffic jams we were finally deposited at 7.30 p.m. on a busy road somewhere; we weren't exactly sure where. It was also now dark. There ensued a slightly anxious half-hour walk using a phone app which took us through the centre of the town. At 8 o'clock, to our great relief, we were at the Daher Guest House but…there was no answer when we rang the bell. I tried calling the number but discovered that my phone wasn't working in Israel. Yim Soon attempted to send a message but she couldn't pick up any wifi and her phone was running out of battery. We had a *very* anxious half-hour until, by chance, Yim Soon found a man around the corner who was the uncle of the guest house owner. The nephew appeared a few minutes later and nonchalantly let us in but by that time my nerves were in pieces. I reminded myself wryly of those words of Nathanael in St John's Gospel, "Can anything good come out of Nazareth?" And, as often at the start of a pilgrimage, I was wondering what could possibly be spiritual about the experience.

I could look back on it all with a smile as I sat with a cup of tea (made with milk even!) on the roof terrace of the guest house and looked out over the town where Jesus and his family had lived. I reflected that if it's true, as the Arabic saying goes, that the hour before dawn is sent from paradise, then the hour after it certainly is too. When I'd gone into the Basilica earlier I was excited to pass a group of Koreans having their photo taken next to a big statue of Mary. And the atmosphere inside the building was peaceful and prayerful. With all the frustrations of the previous day's journey, I had an overwhelming sense of goodness in that holy place. Was that the actual site, as is claimed, where the angel Gabriel appeared to Mary? That didn't really matter to me at that moment.

Our ten-mile walk from Nazareth took us to Cana, where we arrived at about 4 o'clock. We could have arrived much sooner but we started late and were on the receiving end of various acts of kindness en route. I had been joined on the roof terrace at 7.30 a.m. by Yim Soon for a sumptuous spread of pitta breads and pastries, with houmous and cream cheese and salad. It was taken with strong Arabic coffee, followed by a cup of tea with milk which was surprisingly tasty even if served in a glass!

We visited the Greek Orthodox Church of the Annunciation, which is built over a spring that is said to have fed the well where the angel Gabriel appeared to Mary. It was packed with pilgrims. So, by that time, was the Basilica of the Annunciation, said to be the site of Mary's house. It was 10.30 a.m. and already hot before we were finally on the Jesus Trail. It took us through the Old City and then up, up and up. There were 460 steps to be ascended, at the top of which was a stunning view over Nazareth and to the hills and valleys beyond. From there we passed through the suburbs, following the yellow marks helpfully painted on telegraph poles. One car stopped in the middle of the road, with the driver asking if we needed a lift anywhere. As we passed a high school, we chatted with some teachers who were outside taking a break from their charges.

We were eventually in open fields, some of them with olive or pomegranate trees. By mid-day, the temperature had reached 30 degrees and the walking became tougher, with scanty shade to be found anywhere. On a stretch along dusty tracks, a huge earth mover stopped by us and the driver threw open the door. Speaking only Arabic he handed us two bottles of cool water (our own supplies were decidedly warm by that point) and even offered us coffee! We gratefully took the water and I managed one of my few words in Arabic, *shukran*, thank-you; probably the most important word of all.

After a few miles of gradual ascent, we were in the small town of Mashhad for a late lunch and from there it was all downhill into Cana. As we entered the town, a car pulled up alongside us driven by an elderly man who enquired what we were doing. He followed that up with an invitation to come into his home. We were warmly welcomed by him, his wife and his sister-in-law. The latter set about making drinks. Firstly, there was the most delicious, freshly made lemonade I will ever have. Then there came strong Arabic coffee, accompanied by chocolate bars. I told our guests how happy I was. The man said, "I happy also!"

It was a short way after that to our accommodation. We were staying at the Cana Wedding Guest House, which is strategically placed right next to the Cana Wedding Church. The exact site of Jesus' first miracle, where he turned water into wine at a wedding feast, is unknown. It seems that the church in Cana is one of four contenders! It even has in the basement one of the supposed original stone jars. As has always been the case with pilgrimage, there would be economic advantage for a town that possessed any kind of holy site. And modern-day Cana is doing a roaring trade in Cana Wedding Wine!

As it happened, the Arabic couple who ran the guest house were celebrating the following day their 55th wedding anniversary. There was more freshly made lemonade on arrival. And we ate a huge and delicious evening meal in their kitchen, so too an enormous breakfast. Then we went to the Church for a 9 o'clock Mass in English. It was being said for a group from Texas that contained several couples who were there to renew their wedding vows. Thanks to a Vietnamese nun we'd spoken to the day before, we had manged to get ourselves on the list. So it was that we were in the line of couples who processed up the aisle to the tune of Mendelssohn's Wedding March. And it was incredibly moving when, as instructed by the priest, Yim Soon and I looked at one another in the eyes and said our 'yes' again. A woman in the row behind us took my phone and demanded a kiss. We willingly obliged.

The renewal of our wedding vows in the Wedding Church of Cana had been a pretty special moment. And then it was rucksacks on backs, and on the road again. Up the steep hill out of the village, passing two elaborately painted mosques. It was another scorchingly hot day, and I didn't mind at all that we missed a bit of an old Roman road on the way. I was just grateful to reach our destination which was the Lavi Kibbutz Hotel. The complex included a swimming pool and sauna which felt like a particular luxury after our long hike. Back in our room, I revelled in being able to drink a cup of tea with milk whilst watching the sun go down over the valley beyond. I was fascinated to then be in the vast dining room surrounded by Jewish families who seemed to come from every tradition of Judaism. There followed a bit of a tense evening as we attempted to plan our route to Tiberias for the next day. The young woman on reception spoke perfect English (having grown up in England!) and was extremely helpful.

That third and final day of walking was, as expected, tough going in the heat. The plan had been to leave Lavi Kibbutz at 7.30 a.m. straight after an early breakfast, and having stocked up on some provisions, for there would be no shops en route. We also had to make sure we reached a certain place in time to get the last bus to Tiberias which would leave at 1.55 p.m.. From that point, transport would cease and shops would begin to close in preparation for the Sabbath. The first challenge was figuring out which of the various paths to take from the kibbutz. We were helped by a man who had moved there from Liverpool fifty years before to help out during the Yom Kippur war. He pointed us along the right path and also popped into the shop to buy us another bottle of water. By this time it was 8.15 and the temperature was already in the mid-twenties. I was sorely tempted to just take the bus all the way to Tiberias. I was glad, in the end, that we didn't!

We left the Kibbutz complex on a dirt track and were soon going up and over the Horns of Hattin. This is a spectacular twin-peaked volcanic formation which resembles the horns of a bull. At a height of 326 metres, it commands panoramic views. It is also near the site of the Battle of Hattin of July 4th 1187, which was decisive in the history of the Crusades. The army of the Second Crusade had been lured by Saladin away from the springs at Tur'an and were pressing on to Tiberius. It was too late in the day, though, for them to reach the lake, and Saladin's forces had cleverly blocked any retreat to Tur'an. They were forced to pitch camp on a plateau with no water or supplies. Saladin's men were surrounding them and they lit fires in the grass around the almost 20,000 strong Crusader army. This both blinded them and compounded their thirst. The following day, the Crusaders were routed. In the following weeks, almost every Crusader stronghold and port fell, and on October 2nd, Saladin's army reconquered Jerusalem.

We met a father and son near the summit of the Horns who were boiling water for coffee and the son gave us further directions on to Mount Arbel, our goal. In the village of Arbel we got chatting to a couple who had come to spend the Sukkot holiday weekend as part of a group of twenty-five family members. Nathalie was from London originally, David from France. They were impressed that we were walking, and they kindly took us to their house to replenish our water supplies.

We made it to the top of Mount Arbel just before mid-day. Yim Soon wanted to follow a further trail through the park, which would give spectacular views over the Sea of Galilee. I was finished. The temperature now was well into the 30s, there was no shade anywhere and it was like walking in a desert; albeit a beautiful desert. We made a retreat to Arbel, and I was most relieved when the Tiberias bus came along. It was a great thrill to get our first glimpse of the lake down in the valley.

I awoke in our hotel near the waterfront on what appeared to be a peaceful Saturday morning and I had the immense pleasure of seeing the sun rise over the hills on the opposite shore of the lake. Not only was it the Sabbath, it was also still the feast of Sukkot, and we had arranged to rent bikes. The plan had been to cycle around the lake all the way to Capernaum. We only made it as far as Magdala, said to be the home of Mary Magdelene. It was too hot and hilly to do a long cycle. We'd also heard in the Chapel at Magdala the disturbing news that early in the morning, Hamas had launched 50,000 rockets from Gaza into Southern Israel. Hamas fighters had also made incursions into Israel at fourteen points along the border and shot people at random, including many young people who had been attending a music festival near the border. Hundreds had already been declared dead, hostages had been taken, and Israeli Prime Minister Netanyahu had declared the country to be at war.

We cycled back to Tiberias, which was completely quiet and actually very peaceful, with most people staying in their homes in response to the news. We were able to have a restful and enjoyable couple of nights in the town. I swam in the lake, we went to a hot spring, we ate well, we saw spectacular sunsets and sunrises. It was quite idyllic, and it was hard to imagine the terrible events happening elsewhere in the country.

The roads the following day were almost empty, so that we made rapid progress down to Jerusalem, where we had planned to spend three nights. After the tranquillity and beauty of the Sea of Galilee, our arrival by bus in the busy, bustling, noisy concrete jungle which is modern-day Jerusalem was something of a culture shock. As was our first excursion from the hostel, which was to the Old City and the Church of the Holy Sepulchre. It was totally thronged with groups of pilgrims. Some were falling prostrate and kissing a slab of stone near the main entrance. One woman was rubbing two sets of rosary beads on the slab. I assumed it must be the supposed spot of Jesus' burial but didn't much care just at that moment. I discovered later that it's the Stone of Anointing, marking the alleged place that Joseph of Arimathea anointed the body of Jesus prior to burial.

We ventured further into the church. A scrummage of camera wielding pilgrims/tourists were in a queue to kiss an icon of the Madonna. In another part of the church another queue had formed. Exactly what they were queuing to see, we had no idea and decided to give it a miss. That place, I found out later, is the actual position where it is claimed that Jesus was buried. As we were also to discover, it is not the only site in Jerusalem that makes that claim!

The sense of a rather unholy chaos was compounded by the existence of scaffolding in the domed central area. It seems that it was erected in 2016 when the six Christian factions that have a stake in the church decided to set aside their differences so that essential repairs could take place. As is related earlier, sensitivities around this holy site run high and it can be hard to get agreement between the sects on the most basic aspects of the upkeep of the Church. As we'd been entering the Church, Yim Soon had pointed out to me a small ladder on a ledge high up on the front façade. It was apparently placed there as early as 1728. By whom and from which denomination, nobody knows, but no-one has dared move it since for fear of incurring the wrath of another faction. The result is that the so-called 'Immovable Ladder' remains there to this day. I hoped that the scaffolding would not stay in place for as long as the ladder!

I was relieved to get back out and to wander through the narrow streets of the old markets. They were eerily quiet, with most people following government advice to stay at home in the aftermath of the Hamas attacks of the previous day and heightened security. An Arab man outside one shop told us to keep safe and then, rather surreally, invited us in to see his stamp collection! He had some curious specimens, including some stamps issued just as the state of Israel was being created. One had on it the original map that had been proposed by the United Nations, in which, he pointed out, Gaza was considerably larger than the current tiny segment.

I was feeling rather ill at ease with the Holy City and decided to take advantage of our hostel kitchen and to cook a meal. We also needed to do some washing. Whilst in the laundry I got chatting to Daniel from the Czech Republic. I mentioned the word pilgrimage to him and he said, "Oh I did a pilgrimage in Spain." He had walked the Camino Francés, beginning, as I had, in St-Jean-Pied-de-Port. Unlike me, he had gone on to Finisterre and Murcia. Then, feeling like he still wanted to do more, he did a bit of the Camino Primitivo. He explained, "I'm not religious but it was a very spiritual experience. I got to know myself better and about connecting with other people." He had been touched by his encounters with such a range of interesting people and to have the most profound conversations. He remarked as well that many of those walking were at threshold points in their lives and were grappling with certain questions. This added to the sense of people being able to share intimately about themselves. Daniel noted how tough it could be but concluded, "Sometimes there's just a magic that happens." I told him that I couldn't agree more. And then I invited him to have a meal with us. He happily agreed and offered the two tins of tuna he'd bought earlier. I enjoyed shopping for the remaining ingredients in a small store across the road, so too having a bit of banter with the big-bearded American Jew on the check out.

And so it was that our first evening meal in Jerusalem was like many of those we'd had on the Camino. It was tuna with vegetables in a tomato sauce with spaghetti, with a nice bottle of Israeli red, and shared with fellow pilgrims. Daniel told us more about himself, and he later invited another guy, Polish Jan, to join us. He also provided some chocolate for dessert. And, the icing on the cake for me, Jan and I watched some Premier League football on his laptop! It was a thoroughly enjoyable, and, dare I say, holy first evening in the Holy City.

We returned to the Old City in the morning, with Yim Soon having prepared, Korean style, a detailed itinerary of holy places to visit. Mercifully, the weather had cooled so that the temperature was 'only' in the mid-twenties, and pleasant for walking. First on the list was the location, in the Armenian Quarter, of the Last Supper. It was closed! Next to that was the Tomb of David. Several Orthodox Jews were assembled there, one of them chanting from the psalms, and a couple of others swaying from side to side. I found it quite touching. Much more so than when we went later into the Church of St Peter in Gallicantu which is said to be the sight of where Peter denied Jesus three times and the cock crew. There was a relentless stream of international groups of pilgrims being disgorged from coaches and led by their guides into the church to take multiple photos there.

The Basilica of St Stephen, just outside the Old City, was far more peaceful. There was Mass in French at noon, which was quiet and prayerful, and afterwards we sat in the shaded courtyard and had a little snack for lunch. On the way to the Mass we'd gone to the Wailing Wall. We joined the many Jewish people touching the rock and making their prayers of petition. As at the tomb of David, I was very moved to be there. No photos are taken; people are there purely to pray.

And then we were back on the pilgrimage/tourist trail. The first afternoon stop was the church at the Garden of Gethsemani at the bottom of the Mount of Olives. We returned through the Damascus gate, passing through a large group of machine gun wielding Israeli soldiers. We'd hoped to go to the Temple Mount but a subsequent group of soldiers was denying entry to any non-Muslims. We walked instead along the Via Dolorosa. It was one of the places I'd most wanted to see in Jerusalem. Having grown up in the Roman Catholic faith I've marked on Good Friday every year of my life the journey that Jesus made to his crucifixion. Whether or not the Via Dolorosa, Way of Suffering, marks the exact route I have no idea. In any case, I didn't find it an especially prayerful experience, following as is does the narrow alleyways of the Old City. Also, by that time I had tired of wandering round ticking off holy places. We left the Old City through the Jaffa Gate and took the tram back along Jaffa Street to the sanctuary of the Abraham Hostel.

Our hostel was a sanctuary indeed a little later when we heard an air raid siren. An announcement told us that we had ninety seconds to get down to the basement. It seems that ninety seconds is the approximate time it takes for a rocket launched in Gaza to reach Jerusalem! We didn't hang around. In the end, we were allowed back to our rooms after just ten minutes or so. Various rumours had been circulating amongst those who had been assembled in the basement. One was that Ben Gurion Airport had been targeted by rockets. There was quite a sense of anxiety in the city and many people were trying to get out of the country as soon as available flights would allow. Yim Soon and I decided to stay calm and to go out in the evening. The streets in the city centre were almost deserted and nearly all of the restaurants had closed. We were grateful to find a burger place open and took our meal back to the hostel.

After breakfast the next day, we headed back towards the Old City where we hoped to have another go at finding the stations on the Via Dolorosa. The day before, we'd found the first three of what are usually fourteen stations which depict different scenes from Jesus' walk to his crucifixion. This time we got to the eighth but couldn't find No. 9 and I was starting to feel claustrophobic in the narrow, covered lanes and annoyed with the constant attention from the shopkeepers. One rather nice moment was chancing upon an icon shop run by two nuns who were from the order of the Little Sisters of Jesus. We went in and introduced ourselves and they were interested to hear that we'd known some of the Little Brothers of Jesus in London. We spoke of the terrible events in the country. The sisters listened sympathetically as we explained that many flights were being cancelled and that we had no idea whether we'd be able to get out of the country. We bought some of their lovely icons: one for each of our children and one for ourselves. They bid us a safe journey home and assured us of their prayers.

On our first day in the city, we'd met an elderly Jewish couple from New York. The lady had a strong sense of Israel being her spiritual homeland and urged us to visit the Great Synagogue. That was my mission for what was due to be our final day in Jerusalem. I found on the way the wonderfully peaceful Independence Park, where I sat on a bench revelling in the green grass and the trees and the lack of traffic noise. That park was to be something of an oasis for me. The Great Synagogue is nearby and I wanted to check first whether I, as a non-Jew, could go inside. I asked a couple of young guys outside if they spoke English. One of them replied, in a London accent, "I certainly do!" Raph (short for Raphael) had grown up in leafy Hampstead in North London and had moved to Israel when he was seventeen. We had a lovely exchange and he assured me that I was most welcome to go into the synagogue. He also confided to me that he'd known one of the people who had been killed at the music festival. The Synagogue was a hive of activity, with a large group of mainly young American and British Jews organising food parcels for soldiers and families affected by the conflict.

When I left, I was approached by an older man who introduced himself as the President of the Synagogue. His final words to me were, "God bless you." I was deeply touched and was overcome by tears as I walked away. I was touched as well a little later when the big bearded American in the store across from the hostel said as I prepared to leave, *Kol tuv*, which means 'All that is good be upon you,' and *Shalom rav*, meaning 'Lots of shalom (peace) to you.'

If that was to be my final day in the Holy City, how special it was to be leaving with the blessings from those two Jewish men.

I had gone back to the shop to buy food for what I thought would be my final act in Jerusalem; to cook again and invite whoever there was in the hostel dining room who needed a meal to join us. It turned out to be Mark from Florida and Phil from England. Phil was in the middle of making apple crumble with whipped cream which he proceeded to share with anyone who wanted it. And then he took a guitar and did a couple of songs. He passed the guitar to me and I sang for a long time to a very international gathering. Two people from Holland, Wil and Henk told me later that the singing was just what they'd needed to lift the mood. It had been a wonderful evening; marred just a bit by returning to our room to discover that our flight for the next day had been cancelled.

That meant we had another full day (at least!) in Jerusalem ahead of us. On the advice of our children, we booked a flight to Amman for two days' later which we were not sure would actually depart. For the third day running we went to the noon Mass in French at St Stephen's. We also made a first visit to the nearby Garden Tomb, which has claims to be the real site of Jesus' burial, as opposed to the Holy Sepulchre. Whether or not that's true, the garden is another little oasis in the city. There were lots of flowers growing and shaded areas, and a group are on hand to welcome visitors.

When we got back to the hostel I was feeling distinctly out of sorts and I was anxious that we were just waiting around for the Friday Amman flight to be cancelled. I needed a Plan B. Again on the advice of our children, I was in the midst of booking an Israir flight to Athens and then saw that they were cancelling many of their flights. I spotted that Blue Bird Airways (a Greek carrier that I'd never previously heard of) were still running all of their flights out of Tel Aviv. There were seats on their flight to Athens on the Friday. It was expensive but I went ahead and booked. And I felt a weight fall from my shoulders. As it turned out, the Amman flight did indeed get cancelled.

It was a worrying time, with the news unremittingly bad. The death toll was rising by the day, on every side. Gaza's only power plant had run out of fuel. A man in the hostel lobby told us that Hezbollah had launched one hundred drones from Lebanon into the North of Israel. Hamas was still sending some rockets into Israel and Israel was sending rockets back. A British Airways flight had turned back from its descent into Tel Aviv and returned to London. Meanwhile, hundreds of thousands of Israeli troops were gathering on the border with Gaza in preparation for a ground assault. Jerusalem itself was relatively safe but I really didn't want to be there anymore.

I got up early in the morning after a fitful night. I walked in the dark to what was by now my favourite place in Jerusalem, Independence Park. I sat on a bench and listened to the birds in the trees and watched as the sun began to rise. I wandered towards the Old City and near the walls I spotted a Franciscan. Just like when I saw two men early in the morning in Nazareth, I figured that this friar must be going somewhere, possibly to a Mass, and I followed him. He entered the Old City by the, now familiar to me, Jaffa Gate and carried on walking through the labyrinth of narrow alleyways. I carried on following him. I felt like I was in a film, in pursuit of my prey. Eventually he went through a metal gate and the gate closed. I knocked and the door was opened by a nun. I asked if there was a Mass. She explained that the 6.30 Mass was just about to start and that I was most welcome. She led me up the stairs into the lovely little chapel of the Missionaries of Charity, the order founded by Mother Teresa. The friar that I'd followed was the priest and the Mass was in English. It was such a gift to be there. And then just before I left, the sister who'd welcomed me at the gate presented me with four prayer cards of Mother Teresa: two for me and two for Yim Soon. She also spoke a bit about the special but troubled place which is Jerusalem; and about the work of the sisters with poor Palestinian families. She said she hoped we'd get home safely. And assured me of their prayers.

Yim Soon and I decided to go to the airport later in the morning to get some up-to-date information. To our immense relief, our flight to Athens the next day was almost certainly going ahead, and there seemed to be other options too. With our minds more at rest we went for a final visit to the Old City. We prayed again at that most scared of Jewish sites, the Wailing Wall; although, sadly, we were still not allowed into the area around the Temple Mount. Tensions there were even higher than usual, with all of the entrance points guarded by soldiers. We found, however, in the Muslim Quarter another little oasis. It was the Church of St Anne which is said to be the location of the pools of Bethesda mentioned in the Gospel of St John. While Yim Soon went exploring, I had a lie down on a bench under a tree. It was quite silent until there came the sound of the Muslim call to prayer for the start of their holy day. It was loud but there was something hauntingly beautiful about it. It got me thinking about that unique place. The Old City in particular marks the confluence of the three major Abrahamic religions. Jews, Muslims and Christians live and pray there cheek by jowl; and not always peacefully.

A little later I heard the unmistakable sound of a Taizé chant, *Laudate omnes gentes*, coming from the church. A group of Germans were singing and producing spectacular echoes. I joined them and initiated a couple of chants of my own. One of them, sung with Yim Soon, was the Korean version of *Ubi Caritas* that I'd sung with Angela and Julio on my first Camino.

There were a few final special moments on the morning of the day that we did eventually manage to leave. I'd been told the day before by the Missionaries of Charity sister that there would be a Mass in English in the Church of the Holy Sepulchre at 6.30 a.m. As ever, it was a magical time to be up and about. I strolled down the now familiar Jaffa Street, along the route that the tram takes. I sat for a few minutes by the walls of the Old City before entering again through the Jaffa Gate. As I was trying to figure out where to go in the complex of narrow alleyways, a Muslim man approached me. He asked where I was going and when I told him, he invited me to follow him. "Where are you from," he asked. "England," I replied. "Ah, fish and chips!" he exclaimed. And he followed that up with, "I pray for peace; we are all children of Abraham." He was on his way back from mosque prayers, while I was on my way to Mass. A Jewish man possibly on his way to a synagogue went by at just that moment on his bike. It somehow encapsulated the religious melting pot which is Jerusalem.

It was a lovely encounter with the Muslim man. He told me that he was a professor in religious studies. He reached into his wallet and pulled out his card. When I looked at it later, I saw that the address was for an antique shop in the Old City! I smiled, and reflected on how the sacred and the secular are never far apart!

It was a little chaotic in the Church of the Holy Sepulchre, even at that early hour, with something of a conveyor belt of services taking place. A 6 a.m. Mass group, including the Mother Teresa sisters, streamed out of the small sepulchre and the American group I'd tagged onto processed in for our 6.30 a.m slot. We could hear from the other side of the sepulchre the chanting from an Orthodox service. And there was also a Mass in a chapel upstairs in an Eastern language. The sepulchre is where people were queuing up to enter when I made my first visit to the Church. As the priest said to us at the start of the Mass, we were at the place where Jesus was buried and rose again. Is it really that exact spot? Or is it at the Garden Tomb just outside the Old City walls? Is it somewhere else altogether? For me, just like at other popular places of pilgrimage, it wasn't really that important in the end. In any case, I was happy to be there, and for many of those in the group the location was clearly highly significant, with one woman so overcome with emotion that she fell to the ground.

Our stay in Jerusalem had been eventful, albeit not in the way we might have expected. There had been noise, stress, anxiety and frustration. There had also been some magical moments: of stillness, prayerfulness, kindness and connection. Not to mention lots of incredible encounters with a wide range of characters from every spectrum, religious and otherwise. It was all of those things that I would normally expect from a pilgrimage. Added to that there was a tiny insight into the reality of so many people in the world who live in conflict zones and in suspicion of 'the other side.' For the possibilities that pilgrimage had given me, in Jerusalem and elsewhere, to get an intimate glimpse into other cultures, to meet people I wouldn't normally meet, and to receive unexpected gifts, I was immensely grateful.

CHAPTER 7

LOURDES

Yim Soon and I went to Lourdes in 2012 as part of a special trip to mark our 20th wedding anniversary. It was my second time in that famous Marian shrine but the first visit for Yim Soon. She had intended going there in 1987 but an encounter in Italy sent her elsewhere and led ultimately to our meeting each other in Canterbury.

Yim Soon had been travelling in Europe and was in Assisi, the place of St Francis, her favourite saint. She had planned to go from there to the South of France and to Lourdes but she met some people from L'Arche who invited her to visit them in their community in the North of France. She gladly accepted the invitation and spent an enjoyable few days in one of the L'Arche houses in Trosly-Breuil alongside people with learning disabilities. She didn't speak any French so was offered the chance to join the L'Arche community in London and ended up spending a year and a half there. She returned to Korea but wanted to come back to L'Arche and so arrived in Canterbury in May, 1989 and I met her on her first day!

We had booked a room in Lourdes for the couple of nights we spent there in October 2012. A friendly and chatty Algerian woman welcomed us, and I was delighted with the small balcony and the view it gave over the town and to the Pyrenees in the distance. Just as I had been on my first visit to Lourdes I was especially moved to spend time in the grotto area.

It was near that grotto in 1858 that a young local girl, Bernadette Soubirous was out collecting wood when she saw a lady dressed in white. On subsequent visits the lady asked Bernadette to drink from the spring that appeared at the grotto, to pray for sinners and to have a chapel built on the site. When Bernadette spoke of the apparitions she was initially disbelieved by the authorities but four years later the visions were declared by the local bishop to be authentic.

The first miracle had already taken place in 1858 when Catherine Latapie, a thirty-eight-year-old woman with a paralyzed hand, experienced a sudden urge to travel to Lourdes. She met Bernadette at the grotto and dipped her fingers into the spring water and her hand was healed. Since then, 7,000 such healings have been attributed to the intercession of Our Lady of Lourdes, although just seventy have been officially declared as miracles by the Catholic Church. The most recent involved a French nun, Sr Bernadette Moriau who had been using a wheelchair since 1980 due to a spinal condition and went on pilgrimage to Lourdes in 2008. After a blessing for the sick she felt a sudden change in her body and shortly afterwards she began to walk. Her case was investigated by the International Medical Committee of Lourdes who eventually concluded that there was no scientific explanation for the cure. The miracle was duly announced by Bishop Jacques Benoit-Gonin of Beauvais in 2018.

My first time in Lourdes had been in 1986, when a group of four of us set off there from Sheffield straight after our graduation ceremony. We took the train down to London, an overnight bus to Paris, then at Gare d 'Austerlitz we began the long journey South. I still remember clearly our arrival at the station in Lourdes, and the palpable sense of anticipation amongst the large crowds of pilgrims. Some, like us, were there to help; others were coming for what they hoped might be a cure of some kind.

For the first of our two weeks in Lourdes we were *brancardiers*, whose literal meaning in French is 'stretcher-bearers.' John, Tim and I were stationed in a barracks-like building close to the grotto, with high walls and a strictly enforced curfew. Our friend Ann was in separate accommodation for the women. One of the first pieces of information we received from a seasoned *brancardier* was the best place to scale the wall at night! There was great camaraderie and banter amongst the *brancardiers* of different nationalities. Earlier that year there had been a scandal involving adulterated Italian wine and one of the French men drew a picture of a skull and crossbones on a bottle of wine and pointed mischievously at our Italian colleagues! It was also just after the World Cup which had featured Diego Maradona's infamous 'hand of God' goal against England. Tim was fond of greeting our international friends with a nodding fist above his head and the word 'Maradona!'

One of our tasks each day was to take people, many of whom were in wheelchairs, to the spring water bath and to help them undress and enter the water. The senior *brancardier* who instructed us stressed the importance of respecting each person's dignity and he told us to "see without looking." Those words left a deep impression on me and they have been useful in all kinds of situations subsequently.

In common with pilgrimage sites around the world, a whole tourist industry has grown up in the town. Lourdes is particularly packed with cafes, bars, hotels and shops selling a wide array of Mary-related trinkets, many examples of which were on display in my home when I was growing up. My mum had visited Lourdes as a young woman and one of her sisters went there regularly (as well as to the Marian shrine at Medjugorje in Croatia) and would always send us something like a statue of Our Lady with flashing fairy lights. I've always rather liked them. Some people, Yim Soon included, find the commercial aspect of Lourdes a bit tacky and off-putting. I've always felt quite at home with it! Faith is faith, and we all express it in different ways.

I saw a lot of those shops and bars in 1986. For our second week in Lourdes we joined the Liverpool diocesan pilgrimage and to get from our hotel to the basilica and grotto area meant walking through the commercial heart of the town. By day we would be taking part in processions and Masses. By night we would sit outside one of the bars playing songs by The Beatles (I'd brought a guitar with me, as had others) and being bought drinks by an appreciative international audience. I guess it's similar to how pilgrims have been spending their evenings for centuries!

There were other English diocesan pilgrimages taking place at the same time. There seemed to be a bit of friendly rivalry between them, in particular around the question of which one was the most 'rowdy' and there were stories of the occasional young pilgrim needing to be sent home for 'inappropriate behaviour!' One of the things that impressed me most was how those young Liverpudlians I was with (some of whom were a little 'rough around the edges' and very much on the rowdy end of the spectrum) appeared to be transformed when assigned to their caring duties, which might include pushing somebody in a wheelchair in a procession. There was a mutual joy and radiance that was manifest between 'helper' and 'helped.' I came to see later in my own 'caring' work how this mutuality is a fundamental aspect of any relationship.

Cardinal Basil Hume, who led the first Westminster diocesan pilgrimage in the 1990s, used to say that Lourdes turns the world upside down so that we see it the right way up! The Liverpool pilgrimage is much older, having begun in 1923. One of those on that inaugural trip to Lourdes was a man called Jack Traynor. He had not walked since 1915 after being severely wounded during the First World War. Indeed, many people tried to dissuade him from setting off from Lime Street Station in Liverpool, fearing the trip would kill him. On arrival in Lourdes he was taken in his wheelchair to the waters and tipped in. The next morning he was seen sprinting from the hospital to the grotto, with incredulous *brancardiers* in pursuit. A priest suggested that Traynor send word to his wife, but he didn't want to make a fuss so sent the briefest of telegrams: 'Am better- Jack.' The story then goes that in subsequent years the members of Liverpool City Council, refusing to believe in miracle cures, would not stop paying Jack his disability pension, despite him taking up his old job as a haulier.

When Yim Soon and I were there in 2012 we purchased some of the ubiquitous mini plastic bottles on sale and filled them with holy water from the grotto to take back and give to family. It seems that scientific tests have been carried out on that water which have declared it to be 'just water.' However, faith can move mountains and can make miracles happen. And whatever anyone thinks of the shops selling plastic, fairy-lit statues, or indeed of the whole phenomenon of divine apparitions or miracle cures, I would challenge anyone to spend some time at the grotto in Lourdes, especially at night, and not be touched by the sense of peace and prayerfulness. There is certainly something very special, and dare I say, healing and miraculous, about that place.

Fr. Anthony, mentioned in the previous chapter, has gone to Lourdes many times and he thinks of pilgrimage as being a prayer walk and says, as others do, that the journey is as important as getting to the destination. For him, the companions met along the way are an essential part of the experience and he relishes how the group of pilgrims becomes a community through the process of walking and sharing together. His first trip to Lourdes as a sixteen-year-old involved rather an epic journey. Fresh from completing his school O-levels, he met up at Victoria station in London with a group that included children with disabilities that he would be helping. They took the train to Dover, the ferry to Calais, then had a long trip down to the South of France; this being long before the advent of the high-speed TGV. Nowadays when he goes to Lourdes, the group meets at the airport but even if the trip to the shrine itself is much shorter, it is the start of people getting to know one another, to journey together, to form a community: the beginning of the pilgrimage experience. Throughout their time as a group there will be shared meals, much joy and laughter, and many stories will be told. He likens this to the experience of Chaucer's pilgrims on the road to Canterbury.

For their time at Lourdes, the group lives together as a family. People help one another, and the relationships formed with those being cared for make a particular impression on Fr. Anthony. He is also inspired to be so close to the places associated with Bernadette, who was an illiterate girl from a family that had fallen into abject poverty due to the collapse of her father's business. Fr Anthony sees this as a sign of how God often uses those that are seemingly of little importance. There are echoes for him of the words from Paul's Letter to the Corinthians: 'God chooses the foolish to confound the wise.' Fr. Anthony mentions as well that his time at Lourdes, as well as in Jerusalem, has helped him to a deeper understanding of the suffering and healing of Jesus.

In common with Fr. Anthony, Paul Raymond enjoyed the great camaraderie he always found amongst his fellow pilgrims to Lourdes. For him, pilgrimage is something to be done with others, and on each of his three visits he was part of a group from his parish in Liverpool which included some who were deemed 'the sick.' This can cover all manner of physical or psychological ailments. What these people have in common is their belief that they might find healing at Lourdes. Paul has travelled on the famous Jumbulance, the specially adapted bus that takes people with physical disabilities to the shrine. He remembers the excitement around that journey, and the deepening of relationships; so too his strong sense of God's presence in the grotto area. The services were somehow more imbued with meaning, and he was especially moved by the torch-light processions. It was also the first time for him to be together with people from different countries and he recalls how "it felt like being one family." He told me how he would touch the wall of the grotto, made smooth by the hands of countless pilgrims, and how he felt connected with all of those people and with the story of the shrine. The experience was for him "very spiritual."

Lourdes has a particular significance with Irish people of a certain generation. For my mum it was the only trip she ever made outside of Ireland or the UK. And, as mentioned already, I grew up surrounded by Lourdes paraphernalia; also with regular invitations at school to either help on the Jumbulance or to donate money so that others could. One of the dreams of a then eighty-nine-year-old woman called Mamie was to go to Lourdes (another was to meet a bishop!). Mamie was supported by the Irish Chaplaincy Seniors Project, whose manager is the aforementioned Paul Raymond who had a close bond with her, formed over many years of visits and multiple cups of tea. Paul and the team made it possible for Mamie to join the Westminster diocesan pilgrimage to Lourdes in 2019, from which there is a photo of a radiantly smiling Mamie in her wheelchair next to Vincent Nichols, the Cardinal Archbishop of Westminster. Both of Mamie's dreams had come true. She had made it to Lourdes and she had finally met a bishop! Plans were in place for her to go again to Lourdes in July 2022. I visited her in her flat in North London in the May of that year and she was telling me excitedly about the trip and mentioned that Paul had gone there many years before on the Jumbulance. "But," she added, with a look of some bewilderment, "Paul's not sick! I thought you had to be sick to go on the Jumbulance!" Sadly, Mamie died in July 2022 and so didn't get to go again to Lourdes but I'll never forget the image of her and the red-robed cardinal outside the Lourdes Basilica, which sits above the grotto.

Annie and John Judge went to Lourdes for the first time in 1983 and have gone there almost every year since. Their fifth and youngest child Becky was born with brittle bone and needed to use a wheelchair. Annie and John were encouraged by a priest friend to organise a trip with other families who had a child with a disability. John was initially reluctant. He ran a pharmacy, he wondered how they'd be able to afford it, and he didn't know who would look after their four other young children. Then three things happened. A woman arrived in their village who was a locum pharmacist; he received an unexpected tax rebate; and friends in Yorkshire said they would look after the children. John was therefore free to drive the minibus down to the South of France, which he considered to be his main purpose in going.

On that first occasion and every time since, the journey for Annie is an essential part of the experience of going on pilgrimage to Lourdes. She observes how people begin to bond and how the group starts to form into a little community. This process continues during the week. It's helped as well by the daily Mass which Annie considers a central part of the routine. It's a shared activity and is always an inclusive and a joyful occasion. In recent years this Mass has been celebrated by Fr Anthony who is part of the group that goes from Canterbury and who is mentioned above.

Annie and John pointed out that amongst many of the other parents in that first group there was a lot of anger around having had a child with a disability. That trip to Lourdes provided a place of mutual support, where people could see that it wasn't just them that were struggling. There was also some respite for parents due to the presence of helpers in the group. And, in common with people on pilgrimage through the ages, there was a lot of fun and humour. After that first journey in 1983, Annie was rather upset to be asked by a family member whether Becky had been "cured." Annie notes that the real cure that occurred was for the parents.

Annie says that you "catch a bug" when you've been a few times and you just want to keep going back. Becky used to say that it was her "spiritual kick for the year!" Annie has especially enjoyed going to the grotto in the middle of the night. She describes walking down the candlelit, zigzag path and arriving at the cave. "It's very emotional," she says, "a peaceful, special place." She explains that the experience is a little different each year because the group changes but that each time "the whole thing is profoundly emotional, with feelings of spirituality here and there, and it's a lot of fun as well."

I was surprised and touched when I received a message in February 2023 from Séamus, CEO of the LIC, London Irish Centre. The LIC contains, amongst other things, the offices of the Irish Chaplaincy where I was working at the time. Séamus had been in Lourdes to attend a mini retreat for people who go to the shrine as helpers. He had met Annie and my name had cropped up in the conversation. *El mundo es un pañuelo*, the world is a handkerchief!

Also in Lourdes in 2023 was one of the members of the wonderful Irish Chaplaincy team and his story is told here:

…PILGRIMS' TALES…

A Week with Friends

The famous French existentialist philosopher, Jean Paul Sartre once famously said that hell was 'other People.' He must have moved in very different circles from the ones I move in.

I spent Easter week of 2023 in Lourdes as chaplain to a group of six disabled children and fifteen helpers. It was only my second visit there, the first having been in 2019 before the pandemic struck. I was no more at home this time than the last as I don't find being surrounded by seriously ill and disabled people easy to cope with. Still, it doesn't do any harm once in a while to be wrenched out of one's comfort zone and forced to embrace a different perspective on life.

What struck me again that week was the friendliness of the people I met and the dedication of the parents, families and helpers in attending to the 24/7 needs of their charges.

A programme of sorts had been worked out in advance consisting of walks, visits to the grotto and prayer services and Masses. Those not in wheelchairs were able to participate in ball games on the beautiful grassy plane near the river overlooked by the Basilica. The highlight of the week is always the HCPT, Handicapped Children's Pilgrimage Trust, Mass which brings together all the groups from the different countries in a joyous celebration of prayer, word, song, dance and banner-waving.

The 2023 Mass was led by the Merseyside group with the theme of 'Jesus, the Good Shepherd.' The Archbishop of Liverpool, Malcolm McMahon OP, presided and the whole event was such a riot of colour, words, music and dancing that I didn't want it to end. Archbishop Malcolm's sermon to the dressed-up sheep in the sanctuary was the shortest I'd ever heard, consisting of "Baah, baah, baah," to the laughter of everyone present. The gospel according to 'Two Lads from Liverpool,' dressed in Liverpool red and Everton blue, also brought much laughter.

Another highlight was the visit to the small ski resort of Gavarnie in the foothills of the snow-capped Pyrenees, close to the Spanish border and one of the starting points for the famous Camino pilgrimage trail. On our last visit we had seen the mountains through a snow blizzard. This time the weather was warm and sunny, presenting a picture postcard of mountain splendour. We had Mass there in a small church dating back to the Middle Ages, once used by the Knights Templar.

As with my last visit, I met with some old friends I hadn't seen in many years. I was particularly pleased to meet with Fr. Kevin Robinson, former chaplain at HMP Belmarsh and a good friend to Irish prisoners. He was delighted to meet me and told me that I hadn't changed a bit, not even for the better! I also met with Bishop Donal McKeown, bishop of Derry and formerly of my own diocese of Down and Connor.

But my attention was mostly drawn to the many ordinary pilgrims for whom Lourdes is a special place of healing, whether of mind, body or soul. It is hard not to be impressed by the faith of so many people. The theme of our Masses throughout the week was the gift of friendship and how much we rely on each other for so many things. Lourdes seemed to be a very easy place to make friends. If hell was other people for Sartre, I can only conclude that heaven must be all about friends and friendship. Someone once said that it is only with friends that one can have hope in this adventure we call life. I certainly experienced the truth of that remark during my week in Lourdes.

Gerry, Northern Ireland

CHAPTER 8

WALSINGHAM

Just as Yim Soon had almost gone to Lourdes in 1987, I almost went on pilgrimage to Walsingham in 1985 when I was in my second year at Sheffield University. I was due to take part in one of the legs of 'Student Cross' that sets off in Holy Week from different locations and meets up over the Easter weekend in that remote village near the North Norfolk coast. I went down with a severe bout of glandular fever after a busy term of burning the candle at both ends and had to pull out of my participation in 'Northern Leg.' I finally managed to walk to Walsingham in 2023.

It seems that by the 15th and16[th] centuries, Walsingham had surpassed even Canterbury in its popularity as a pilgrimage destination. Royal patronage probably did it no harm. Henry VIII was a regular pilgrim, as was his first wife, Catherine of Aragon. A shine to Our Lady had been established in 1061 following a vision of Lady Richeldis, an Anglo-Saxon noblewoman. Richeldis had an apparition of the Angel Gabriel promising Mary that she would give birth to a son, and was then asked by Mary in this vision to build an exact replica in Walsingham of Jesus' family home. The original was built in simple wood and it led to Walsingham being called the Nazareth of England. The Holy House, together with most of the priory next to it, was destroyed by order of Henry VIII in 1538. Shrines, holy relics and the veneration of saints were banned by Henry due to their association with Roman Catholic beliefs. The practice of pilgrimage likewise was outlawed.

Andy Bull is a walker, journalist and author who has re-created a walk from London to Walsingham which follows some of the way that medieval pilgrims would have taken. In spite of the importance of Walsingham, pre-Reformation, as a pilgrimage site, there is little existing trace of the route that people would have taken from London. By contrast, the (alleged!) ancient pilgrimage routes to Canterbury are clearly marked on Ordnance Survey maps, many country lanes in Kent are named 'Pilgrims Way,' and there are still some pilgrims at least who arrive at Canterbury Cathedral after a long journey on foot. Most pilgrims to Walsingham, on the other hand, tend not to have walked very far at all. Of the 200,000 Catholics who visit the Marian shrine each year, the vast majority will have walked just the final Holy Mile that links the Slipper Chapel outside the village and the ruins of the Abbey.

Andy's route is split into thirteen stages and they are detailed in his book 'London to Walsingham Camino.' I had his guide in one hand and my phone in the other as I got off the train at Brandon in August 2023, hoping I would be able, without a paper map, to follow the directions to Great Cressingham, which was Andy's Stage 10.

The night before my walk I was staying in Norwich with an old friend Mike. On the way to the station in the morning, I was excited to stop at the church of St Julian. We visited there the small 'cell' at the side of the church which was the home for many years of the famous mystic, theologian and writer Mother Julian of Norwich until her death sometime after 1416. I am often quoting to people her most well-known saying: 'All shall be well, all shall be well, and all manner of things shall be well.' As I boarded the train for the fifty-minute journey to Brandon, with the usual bit of apprehension at the start of a new pilgrimage, I prayed that all would indeed be well. As usual, I needn't have worried.

With the sky overcast, the first challenge on leaving Brandon station was trying to determine which direction North was! I figured it out eventually (based on the fact that the train had been heading West) and I was on my way. The route followed dirt tracks for a while and later entered a sizeable forest. On the dirt track I had been comforted to see another set of footprints but in the forest I was totally alone. Indeed, I didn't see any other walkers for the entire day. I managed, with the help of a map on my phone, to navigate my way along a gridiron of grassy forest paths and was relieved to emerge into the village of Mundford. I collapsed against the wall of the village hall, cast off rucksack and boots and had a well-earned sandwich, followed by a little nap on the grass.

The next bit of the route followed the original 'Walsingham Way.' Except that, a few centuries on from when Walsingham was the most popular pilgrimage destination in England, that way is now a busy A-road and with no pavement. I was striding along the right-hand verge as best I could when a van stopped on the other side, with the driver motioning for me to get in. It was hot, the traffic (not to mention the rucksack) was heavy and I willingly did as I was told. As I jumped in, the young man introduced himself as Peter and said he liked to do people a good turn. He was curious as to why I was walking on that busy stretch of highway and asked, "Haven't you got a car?" I explained that I was on pilgrimage to Walsingham and it seemed that he was familiar with neither pilgrimage nor Walsingham. And although I found it rather hard to explain, he appeared to be touched by what I was doing. He was even more touched when I told him I was writing a book and that he was going to get a mention! He had to turn off after a few miles to go and inspect a damaged telegraph pole and left me at a junction. I was relieved to miss the walking on the A-road and grateful to have received my first random act of kindness on the way to Walsingham. I checked my phone and discovered that I was only a couple of miles from The Olde Windmill Inn where I was to spend the night, and I walked those two miles with a broad grin on my face.

After a peaceful night and a 'Club Breakfast' I was back on the road. Before leaving the pub I'd had a little chat with a mother and son who were also setting off to walk to Castle Acre, although their ultimate destination was not Walsingham, rather their home on the coast. I was on my own again on narrow lanes that followed the ancient 'Peddars Way.' Named after the Latin *pedester*, meaning on foot, it is Roman or maybe even older, and it would certainly have been used by pilgrims to Walsingham. Indeed, Catherine of Aragon walked the stretch from South to North Pickenham on March 13th 1517. A few days afterwards, Charles Brandon, Duke of Suffolk, wrote to Henry VIII to inform him that he'd met the queen and accompanied her for the final forty or so miles to Walsingham.

It was on that very stretch between South and North Pickenham that there is a signpost at the side of the road declaring: 'St Mary's-ancient murals.' I made the detour of half a mile along a stony track that ascended alongside a row of trees and suddenly there appeared on the brow of the hill and in a gap between the trees what appeared to be a perfectly preserved church that dates from at least 1090, although possibly as early as the 7th Century. In fact, as I read in Andy's book, it had been derelict, with the roof collapsed, and been used by satanists until it was discovered by chance in 1992. A woman called Gloria Davey spotted it, obscured by ivy, when she was out walking and told her husband Bob about it. He then painstakingly restored it over twenty-five years. He struggled at first to get any financial assistance. Then in 1996 a piece of Victorian plaster fell from the wall to reveal 1,000-year-old murals. There was a visit from the then Prince Charles, grants were awarded, and Bob received an MBE.

The church is opened for a couple of hours in the afternoons, so with it being 10.30 a.m. it was closed. I was joined outside by a lady called Chick who had also seen the sign and had driven up the makeshift track in an open-top car, together with her two dogs. We got talking and when it emerged that my wife was Korean she said, "Well, fancy that; have a look at what I'm reading at the moment!" And she produced from her bag a book by a North Korean woman who had defected to the South. I produced from my rucksack the book I was reading, which was one by a South Korean woman! From there we got onto the subject of my own books and she was interested in my recently published second book. I happened to have one with me and was happy to give it to her, with the message, 'Dear Chick, lovely to meet you on my pilgrimage to Walsingham.'

We got onto discussing the chance but remarkable meetings that we have when out and about. I mentioned the Spanish man who said to me on my first Camino, "El mundo es un pañuelo." Chick said, "Oh, I've got a story that illustrates that perfectly." She had once been sitting on a park bench in London and a young

Australian woman sat next to her and they got chatting. Chick mentioned that her daughter had spent some time in Victoria and when she said her name, Zia, the young woman exclaimed, "She was my flat-mate!"

We spoke for ages: about our children, our travels, my impending move to Ireland, about people with learning disabilities, about the origin of Walsingham as a pilgrimage destination. Before I eventually had to start walking again, I declared to her, "You never know who you're going to meet on pilgrimage; and it's precisely these kinds of encounters that make it for me."

The walking was quite tough going from there on, although when I reached the village of North Pickenham I was on the receiving end of another random act of kindness. A woman came out of her house and asked if she could refill my water bottle and I gratefully accepted. But then I managed to somehow deviate from the path coming out of North Pickenham. The Andy Bull route follows a dead straight Roman way (which I was excited about being on) but I ended up on a not quite so straight non-Roman road which must have added a couple of miles to the walk and which also meant an unpleasant trek along the verge of the extremely busy A47. I tried to remind myself that taking unplanned detours is all part of the pilgrimage experience. But I was still a bit annoyed with myself.

I finally spotted in the distance the impressive ruins of the Norman castle, from which Castle Acre gets its name and I arrived at the Village Hall just in time to be let in at the agreed time of 3 p.m. When I'd been planning accommodation for the walk, Castle Acre was all booked up with it being the August bank holiday weekend and I was almost resigned to sleeping rough. I'd thought that one night of that wouldn't kill me. Until, that is, I'd seen that the weather forecast was for rain. I discovered that a Student Cross group sleep in the hall every year and I was given special dispensation by the Hall Committee to stay overnight, after explaining that I was on pilgrimage to Walsingham and writing a book. I was very glad to have a roof over my head, also to have the chance to make a cup of tea. One of my first acts on arrival in the village was to buy milk in the shop; and I'd brought some teabags from home. I sat out in the garden of the hall, which overlooks the imposing castle walls and moat. I had two cups of tea and a scone. And rarely will tea and a scone taste as good as they do after a walk of fifteen miles.

The next day's walk would take me to Fakenham, which would leave a short last stretch to Walsingham. Special things usually seem to happen on the final day before reaching a pilgrimage destination and my final day before getting to Walsingham was to be no exception.

I'd left the Village Hall in Castel Acre at 6.45 a.m. and relished walking in the cool of the morning. I had five or six miles done on the quiet country lanes before stopping for breakfast in the village of Litcham. I bought a chicken and bacon bap in the shop and was grateful to also be given a maple and pecan Danish for free as it had gone past its sell-by date. I sat and ate them on the village green as the sun began to rise above the haze. As on previous days, I met no other pilgrims but had nice chats with some dog walkers going across the fields near the abandoned medieval village of Godwick. Towards the end of the walk, I went into the church of St Mary in Colkirk and was thrilled to see an entry by Andy Bull in the visitors' book, dated April 2023. He had signed himself 'Pilgrim from London to Canterbury.'

I finally arrived in Fakenham after the sixteen-mile trek and made for The Crown in the centre of town where I cast off boots and socks and tucked into a tuna mayo baked potato. As at Castle Acre, there had been no room at the inn in Fakenham, and I still had a bit over three miles to go to my bed and breakfast in the village of Great Ryburgh. I didn't fancy going there along the road, which was the route recommended by one of my phone apps. I spotted on another app a dismantled railway line which crossed the river Wensum and appeared to lead to a footpath that went directly to the village in question. I set out through the town. I found the old railway line and I followed it down to the bridge crossing the fairly wide river but it was completely overgrown further on. I spotted a path running along the river and thought that I could surely wade across and pick up the path on the other side. That was easier said than done. In the first place where I tried to cross, the water was shallow to start with but got deeper and deeper and muddier and

174

muddier so that I was submerged almost to my waist. I made a hasty retreat and saw that my phone had got a bit wet.

I managed to cross at a different spot but was then into a field that grew thicker and thicker with nettles and thistles. And, to my dismay, there was another river (I was told later that it was a parallel drainage ditch!). It was not as wide but it was still quite deep. I chose a spot where there was an overhanging branch on the other side, removed boots and socks once more, and took my chance. I survived again but was into more nettles, followed by a thicket of trees. Once out of there I was in a field of sheep and beyond that there was a track which, I assumed, must lead to a road. To discover which road exactly I would need my phone but I was horrified to see that it wasn't working. How reliant we have become on our phones! I carried on regardless up the track, by which time it was starting to rain quite heavily. Not that it mattered too much to me as I was wet anyway! At the end of the track a car was waiting for me, and in it the landowner through whose land I had passed illegally! When I explained my situation, she was actually quite understanding and gave me directions to Great Ryburgh. It was still a good distance off and I was so relieved to finally arrive, sodden and tired, at 'Melody House.'

There was a small chip shop in the village and I planned to eat my portion in the churchyard. The church itself was open and I peeped inside to see lots of people seated at tables which were filled with glasses of wine. I was rather envious of the convivial atmosphere, and thought that it would have been nice to have had some company on my final evening before Walsingham. As I made to sit on a bench amidst the graves, a man passed by and I asked what was happening in the church. He explained that it was a wine tasting and he was serving the food. The evening was being hosted by the son and widow of a famous French wine taster. He went on to say that I was welcome to come to the kitchen to eat my fish and chips and to have a beer. I gladly accepted the invitation and sat as he, Peter, together with Anne and Tony got various dishes ready. They found time as well to listen to my escapades in getting to their village! Anne was interested to hear that I was on pilgrimage and explained that they kept camp beds in the hall for passing pilgrims. They had also had Andy Bull with them three weeks previously.

When I finished eating, I asked Anne if I could help with anything and was put into service bringing some of the dishes round the tables. And then when all the food had been sent out, Anne said, "Right, it's time for us to go and do some tasting!" I was sat down at a table at a spare place which had six glasses of red wine ready to be tasted. And I had the most magical time with the people at that table. I spoke most with a couple who had been married for forty-six years: Angelino, originally from Sicily and Janet, a local woman. They had come with their daughter Alessandra and her husband Ollie. And there was also Paul and Elaine, another local couple. They were all tickled to hear both my story of getting across the rivers, and my just happening to have been in the churchyard with my fish and chips on the last night of my pilgrimage to Walsingham and ending up at a wine tasting!

I woke early the next morning and was out strolling in the village and rejoicing in the reddish sky and the coolness in the air following the rain. I was feeling at peace as I came to the end of my little pilgrimage. And as I went past the church of St. Andrew, I fondly recalled again the completely unexpected but wonderful events of the evening before.

I caught a taxi to the parish church in Fakenham and began the last of the six miles to Walsingham. I paid a brief visit to the Church of All Saints in East Barsham, where Heny VIII is known to have passed through on at least one of his many pilgrimages. After only an hour I was already at the Church of St Giles in Houghton St Giles and, by chance, just in time for the 10 a.m. communion service. I was a mere mile from Walsingham and way ahead of schedule so decided to join the other five members of the congregation plus the priest. It was a fitting way to mark the end of my pilgrimage and there was pleasant chat after the service over delicious coffee and shortbread biscuits.

A short way down a narrow lane from the main road is the Slipper Chapel, which forms part of the Catholic Shrine. By some little miracle, the Slipper Chapel was left alone by Thomas Cromwell in 1538 after he had completely destroyed the Holy House down the

176

road and it had a variety of uses over the centuries, including a poor house, a forge, a cowshed and a barn. It was bought in 1896 by a woman called Charlotte Boyd who gifted it to the Roman Catholic Church for renewed liturgical use. In 1934 it became the National Shrine of Our Lady.

I said a little prayer in the Slipper Chapel and then, just as Henry VIII would have done five centuries before, took off my shoes and socks and set off along the Holy Mile. I have to confess that I was feeling a little bit smug about it as cars and cyclists passed me on the narrow road, aware that barefooted pilgrims have always been regarded with particular esteem! At the famous pilgrimage site of Lough Derg in Co. Donegal the usual practice is to spend a twenty-four-hour vigil on the island: praying, fasting and…walking around in bare feet. My mum told me how purified she felt after doing this as a young woman. Likewise, as explained in the next chapter, many pilgrims walk barefoot up Croagh Patrick in Co. Mayo. I have three times made the stony ascent of Ireland's Holy Mountain, in stout walking boots each time, and can attest to how painful it must be to do it barefooted. I suppose the idea, as old as pilgrimage itself, is that the greater the pain, the greater the penance; and therefore the greater the heavenly reward!

I don't know what state the Holy Mile road would have been in back in Henry's time. Now it's tarmacked with just a few bits of grit here and there. It wasn't such a terrible penance!

I finally made it into Walsingham in my bare feet. I was aware that the arrival at the destination is often for me something of an anticlimax. I was glad enough to enter the grounds of the Anglican shrine where I was to spend the night. Like the Roman Catholic shrine, this was re-established in the 1930s. It was part of an Anglo-Catholic revival in the Church of England and instrumental in the excavation of the old shrine and the creation of the new was Hope Patton who was the vicar in Walsingham at the time.

Many parish groups come to spend a weekend at the shrine. One such is that of St. Paul's in Camden in London, and one of those who goes regularly is Mary. She says it's somewhere that she feels close to Mary and to God, also to the many other pilgrims who have journeyed there over the centuries from far and wide. For

Kathryn too it's a special place, and she is especially touched to take part in the Stations of the Cross.

James, an Anglo-Catholic priest in the Church of England, is vicar of St. Pauls. He went to Walsingham for the first time in 1993 when he was a student and helping out on a children's pilgrimage. A vivid memory for him is the coach from London dropping them all off at the Slipper Chapel. As I had done in 2023, they took their shoes off and walked barefoot along the Holy Mile. And like me, their journey ended at the Holy House in the Anglican shrine, which had been rebuilt, in brick, in 1938. It is a special site for James, dark and lit only by candles. He loves the sense of intimacy and finds it womb-like, with the image of Mary as the focal point. Indeed, Walsingham is for him "a place to go and see mother!"

James has gone back with groups every year since and he marvels at how people are changed by the experience. He sees people being renewed in their personal faith, and he notices a spiritual energy that simply permeates everything. People from all walks of life are brought together in a profound way. They help one another, and in the shared meals people let down their guards. There are no barriers. As a final thought, James remarks how the local economy is almost exclusively shrine-related. In the intertwining of the sacred and the secular, Walsingham is no different from pilgrimage sites the world over.

Following my own arrival at the Anglican shrine, I had a few hours until my room would be ready so sat in the pristine and peaceful gardens and had a sleep on a bench. I went into the Shrine Chapel and visited the Holy House. It left me rather unmoved, and I thought, "Is that it?" Perhaps it was yet another classic case of initial disappointment at the destination. I could see, however, that with its massed rows of candles and image of Mary it would be a place of great comfort for many. At 2.30 p.m I joined the daily procession of pilgrims getting sprinkled and blessed with water from the well that was discovered when work on the shrine began in 1931. It's interesting to note that part of the vision of Lady Richeldis in 1061 had been of a spring bubbling up through the ground!

One of the many priests present gave some helpful words of reflection in which he referred to that sense of disappointment we might feel on finally coming to a sacred place and also the challenge of returning to 'the real world.' I was glad to be there with that motley crew of humanity, each of us searching for something. I also enjoyed taking part in the Evening prayer in the shrine chapel, and was touched when a young priest gave me a book so I could follow the service.

I'd wandered a bit in the village in the afternoon, and was kindly allowed in to see the impressive ruins of the old priory and with no charge. I saw the site of the original Holy House, completely destroyed in 1538. On that spot a Mass was about to take place. In the rain! I meandered out of the priory and watched as other pilgrims were coming to the end of the Holy Mile. A group of students from Durham University came along in their bare feet and went into the Roman Catholic church. As well as Anglican and Roman Catholic centres, there is also in the village a Methodist Chapel and even a Russian Orthodox church in the old station house! I was reminded a bit of Glastonbury: different faith traditions living cheek by jowl in a place of great spiritual significance.

Student Cross began in 1948 when Wilfred Maundcote-Carter organised a 'Cross Carrying Pilgrimage of Penance and Prayer.' Thirty male Catholic students and chaplains walked from London to Walsingham during Holy Week carrying a large wooden cross. Maundcote-Carter was inspired by and sought to replicate the British Peace pilgrimage of 1946 to Vézelay in France which was the first event organised after the war by the justice and peace group Pax Christi. Vézelay had been the site where in the twelfth century, Bernard of Clairvaux had spoken to pilgrims on the theme of reclaiming Jerusalem, which was a precursor of the Second Crusade. Pax Christi, by contrast, declared their walk to be a 'Reparation Crusade' or a 'Peace March' and there were fourteen separate legs, each carrying a cross. They came from Britain (via Dieppe), Luxembourg, Italy and various places in France. The pilgrims walked without food or transport and 40,000 people flocked to greet them at Vézelay. They were assisted on their arrival by the Boy Scouts of France who set up tents. The walkers included German prisoners of war who carried two pieces of wood formed into a fifteenth 'peace cross.'

That 1948 walk to Walsingham was intended to be a one-off event but it was such a success that the participants said to one another at the end, "Shall we do it again next year?" In 1949, a second group walked from Nottingham and this came to be known as 'Northern Leg,' and was the one I almost joined in 1985.

It was also in 1985 that my friend Gabs heard about Student Cross for the first time when she was a new student at Sheffield. When she went home for Christmas she tentatively told her parents that she was planning to do it during Holy Week of '86. "Oh, we've done that ourselves," they said, to her surprise. Her dad had done Northern Leg in 1958 when at Manchester University and he had walked with a man called Neil who was to become his brother-in-law. His wife-to-be, Neil's sister, did a one-day pilgrimage to Walsingham in the early 1960s called Graduate Cross. She was one of the first three women to be allowed to walk on what had hitherto been an all-male event: the only catch being that those three brave females were not allowed to walk all the way and they had to do the cooking! They were also not allowed to carry the cross! Gab's mum complained and was eventually allowed to carry the (lighter) end of the cross!

There was still quite a gender imbalance by 1986. Gabs was one of just five women with twenty men. Another of the five was Alison Gelder who had just married Ian. Both of their walking exploits are mentioned in the Rome chapter of this book.

Gabs has gone to Walsingham many times since and has enjoyed the walks of fifteen to twenty miles per day and the talking to people en route. Due in part to it taking three to carry the cross, she discovers her dependence on other people. Walking alone would be much harder, she thinks. Carrying that large wooden cross alone would be impossible. She is also pushed to her limits at times with, amongst other things, the sleeping on the floors of church halls. She recalls on one occasion not being able to find her towel and wanting to burst into tears. At which point Alison said, "You can borrow mine." I know from my own experience of pilgrimage the significance of such small acts of kindness.

Gabs enjoys the singing on the way, which by all accounts includes a certain repertoire of rude songs which are performed year after year in pubs at the end of the day after a few drinks. It also includes spiritual songs which are used in the daily liturgies. Gabs, in common with many, mentions how creative and inspiring these liturgies are, especially on Good Friday at Walsingham when all the legs come together, and on Easter Sunday. She appreciates as well the times of stillness. And in common with others, she enjoys the fun and the laughter.

Walking with people who are different, Gabs encounters alternative viewpoints to her own and this helps her to see things in a different way. She loves walking through and looking at the countryside; and she appreciates that others might spot something that she doesn't. She loves the camaraderie, so too the opportunities for reflection. She admits that this annual event has kind of taken over her life. She views the carrying of the cross as symbolic of the fact that, whether we like it or not, there is an element of suffering on pilgrimage and indeed in our lives generally. This mirrored the little insight I had in Santiago in May 2023 when I remarked to Hanne and Jan that in some mysterious way suffering was an essential part of the experience.

Like Gabs, John heard about 'Northern Leg' at Sheffield, and in common with her he continues, with all of the hardships involved, to walk every year.

...PILGRIMS TALES...

How I Learnt to be a Pilgrim

I was in my first year at university when a friend suggested that since I liked walking and singing I would enjoy a pilgrimage to Walsingham. I certainly had the stamina for walking long distances: my friend was right in that respect. But he didn't tell me what else a pilgrimage might entail: blisters, sleepless nights, a stomach that wondered where the next meal was coming from. Nor did he explain that the group would be carrying a large wooden cross in remembrance of Christ's journey to Calvary and covering about 120 miles.

I had the idea that people had done pilgrimages in the Middle Ages to atone for their sins and I knew nothing of the history of Walsingham or how it had drawn people from all over Europe. Slowly, I began to see myself following in a long tradition of journeys on foot, taking in beautiful and wild landscapes and contemplating nature as a place to meet God.

Just as I had learned from the Sheffield University Catholic Chaplaincy that religion could have a social side, the group were encouraged, even expected to socialise in the evening in pubs. That was fine for me, as I was used to hearing music in bars in Ireland, and at various Chaplaincy events. I brought an Irish song but having the spotlight fall on me was a new experience. Even more so when we were supposed to share our thoughts with the group in a 'station' on the road. I remember us sheltering in the middle of a storm in a remote barn on the Fens and being astonished that the group listened to me and my thoughts about Zaccheus, the little man who wanted to see Jesus but thought he wasn't good enough. Perhaps there was a parallel with my own feelings of unworthiness.

My first pilgrimage was also a time to learn that people are imperfect, even a group of Christians, and that sometimes there was selfishness appearing where I expected holiness to be. For instance, making sure you got the best spec for your sleeping bag seemed a priority for some and it disheartened me. Compounded with lack of sleep (I would lie there at night judging who was the loudest snorer!), a dodgy tummy and painful blisters, I decided we really did have something to atone for.

Holy Week of 1982 also saw the events leading up to the Falklands War and opinions were split over Britain's conflict with Argentina. We passed one day by a missile base in deepest Norfolk, and that gave us plenty of food for thought about wider selfish and destructive acts.

Arriving in Walsingham meant meeting other groups who had travelled on equally long routes to the shrine and an experience of fantastic music and liturgy for the Easter Triduum. It was only then that I discovered we weren't all Catholic, and remembered that the Masses we'd celebrated en route, including the one in a pub, had been openly shared with others of different beliefs.

The whole experience had pushed me to my limits, and it would be two years before I repeated it, this time with Kettering Leg from Northamptonshire. Later still, I found my favourite route, Essex Leg from Colchester, and, later still, I had a brief, self-indulgent avoidance of the weight of the big crosses and chose the lightweight one of Midland Leg. All this time, I was gathering lifetime friendships which extended to reunions all over the country, all infused with the pilgrim spirit that lights up the people we meet.

It brought me to understand I was really on the great pilgrimage of life. That is to say I gradually came to see the importance of journeys in life: meeting people on the way and learning from each other. I have been helped through pilgrimage to develop deeper relationships, to be part of a group, to lead others in their own discovery of the experience (having never seen myself as a natural leader) and to appreciate the innate kindness of human beings. I'm struck to see the network of friends which has grown out of what was originally such a simple journey. What a powerful experience it has been.

John, England

Ian and Kate are other friends who have been going to Walsingham for many years. Similar to Gabs, Kate says, "I can't think of doing Easter any other way," and, also in common with

Gabs, Ian adds that, "It's addictive!" It's the people that make it for Kate, and it is a sacred week in the year for her.

Ian did Student Cross for the first time in 1984 when he was a student at Sheffield and has taken part almost every year since. The essence for him is "community and acceptance." He sees how new people are welcomed easily into the group each year and how they bring their own unique stories. Kate notices how everyone seems really alive and she finds the daily services uplifting and the singing amazing. On Kate's first Student Cross she knew she had made friends for life and she always enjoys being out in the flat, East Anglian fens and being able to see for miles. And for her, "Nothing beats that final walk into Walsingham." When she arrives in the Slipper Chapel she can virtually smell the generations of pilgrims. She spends five minutes in front of the statue of Our Lady of Walsingham and she never fails to feel emotional.

Ian and Kate love how their children have grown up with this annual pilgrimage to Walsingham, and I was touched when I heard that their younger daughter Lucy was a group leader in 2023. In her group was that veteran Student Crosser and long-distance walker Alison Gelder; also my friends Paul and Jenny. For Lucy, Walsingham is "the most special place," and the arrival there on the Friday evokes powerful emotions. She is moved by the peacefulness and the joyfulness she finds there. She looks forward every year to being with such a special group of people and to having such a unique experience.

She enjoys the walking too and observes how everyone in the group looks out for one another. "Everyone's in it together," she remarks. Lucy is also touched by the lovely comments that are made by people that they pass on the streets. Those people seem to look forward to the group arriving each year during Holy Week and they appear in turn to be touched. This mutual giving and receiving echoes my experience on the Camino. I can also relate to Lucy's observation that pilgrimage takes you into another space, where one becomes a bit more aware of the natural world and of the people one is with.

Like Lucy, Gabs' daughter Tabitha has grown up with the pilgrimage to Walsingham. As a young child she was with her family on 'Pegleg,' a family-friendly group which had been started by Ian and Alison in 1992. Later she took part in 'Wensum leg' which had been set up for teenagers. She recalls having no embarrassment about walking through villages in a hi vis jacket whilst carrying a cross because she was doing it with friends of a similar age. The week is like a retreat for her. It gives her time to reflect, she enjoys both the beautiful countryside and the laughter and the 'in-jokes', and she feels close to God.

What began in 1948 as a one-off walk from London to Walsingham with thirty men carrying a heavy wooden cross comprises now ten different routes, seven for adults and three for families. The three hundred participants vary in age from tiny babies to people in their eighties, and include people of all faiths and none. In order to reflect this growing diversity, the pilgrimage was renamed in 2021 as 'Pilgrim Cross.'

I was happy that I'd finally had the chance to spend some time in Walsingham, England's Nazareth. Happy as well that I'd been able to walk some of the way that friends of mine have been walking faithfully every year for decades; and that pilgrims of old were walking for centuries in their hundreds of thousands. On my final morning there I attended an early Mass in the Shrine Chapel which was simple and prayerful. I had breakfast in the refectory amidst the dozens of pilgrims who would be taking part in a big healing service during the day. I chatted with Mary from Yorkshire, another frequent visitor, and asked what was important about the place for her. She said that Walsingham was as close to Lourdes that she could get to without having to go to Lourdes. She added that she loved the sense of peace in the shrine. And her final words were, "I can leave all my worries here…well, almost all of them."

Chairs were being arranged on the lawn for the healing service as I went on my way. For me, as ever, the journey had been at least as important as the destination. I was extremely grateful for all I'd been given on that journey, and also for the chance to be leaving well. And there was one final question in my mind. Had I, in common with others, been changed by the experience? On reflection I think that, yes, in some mysterious and almost imperceptible way, I may well have been.

CHAPTER 9

CROAGH PATRICK

I checked the weather forecast for what was to be my third time going up Croagh Patrick, Ireland's Holy Mountain. It wasn't looking great. There was due to be heavy rain in the morning, then lighter rain from midday but with the possibility of thunder and lightning.

I wasn't going to miss it so decided to wait until eleven o'clock before making the short drive over from Westport where I was staying to the starting point. Also, I'd told lots of people that I was going to do it. One was a Galwayman called Pádraig who'd I'd met in London and who told me he walks up every year. "There's just something about it," he said, and he went on to tell me that he especially loves doing it on 'Reek Sunday.' On that, the last Sunday in July, 25,000 people climb the mountain, some in bare feet and some on their hands and knees. Indeed, a few people had asked if I was planning to walk up in my bare feet! No, I wasn't! The sharp stones on the final steep ascent are tough enough even in strong walking boots. Pádraig remarked that it was great to sense that those stones have been trodden by so many for such a long time. On a clear day, he surmised, you could almost reach out and touch heaven from the top.

Until fairly recently, it was common to walk up Croagh Patrick at night. John, another Galwayman living in London, recalled that of the five occasions he had walked up it in his earlier years, three of them had been in the dark. "Did you use a torch?" I asked. "If you had one!" he replied. "And if you could afford a stick, you'd use one of them too!" He went on to add that the stick would then be sold afterwards to another pilgrim. I found it hard to imagine scrambling up those steep inclines in the pitch black. "You had to be careful!" John pointed out.

I'd been happy to have bright, clear days on my first two times on The Reek, the popular name for the mountain and which simply means high hill in Irish. The second ascent was five years previously and I'd been on a bit of a sacred mission in the West of Ireland. I'd been to Glenamaddy in Galway, near to which my dad was born and raised. I was visiting my Aunty Nellie who was the last surviving member of the family there. It was only the second time we had met and the first time we had actually spoken to each other: a long story, but one with a happy and a healing ending. It was a lovely visit, with bountiful tea and cake and then a walk across a couple of fields to see the old croft house where dad was born. It's a single-storey dwelling (now used for storage) with a central kitchen area and two small rooms either side, and that was home to a family of seven. It was very touching for me to finally see the house, so too the graveyard where my paternal grandparents are buried. Both of them died before I was born.

After spending a night in Clifden on the Atlantic coast, I'd driven up through the vast, rugged, beautiful wilderness of Connemara into Mayo and towards the Holy Mountain. It is so called because St Patrick is said to have gone there during the Lent of 441 AD and spent forty days and forty nights at the summit, praying, fasting and doing penance. At 764 metres above sea level it is Ireland's highest point and it is also the place from which Patrick banished the snakes from Ireland by chasing them into the sea. As with many sacred Christian sites, it had spiritual significance in pre-Christian times. The village of Murrisk which lies at the foot of the mountain is where the pagan harvest festival of Lughnasa was celebrated. Today, Murrisk is the site of the National Famine Memorial.

I was lucky with the weather that day and had incredible views down over the estuary going out into the Atlantic, and the little islets dotted about. The picture I took of Clew Bay was to be used on the cover of my first book *Looking Ahead with Hope*.

I met a lot of interesting people on the way. There were a couple of Irish guys who were walking up The Reek for the thirty-fifth time, an Australian woman whose family had come from Mayo, a young French couple who shared their coffee with me at the top. Following perhaps the example of St Patrick, as well as pilgrims through the ages, some people who walk Croagh Patrick do so in a spirit of penitence. I would say that I was doing it more in a spirit of thanksgiving.

Five years on and the rain was lashing down as I stood in an ominously empty car park. It had been pouring the day before when I'd been back in Galway making another visit to Aunty Nellie. We'd gone again to the graveyard to visit my paternal grandparents. And, back at the bungalow, we'd feasted on soda bread and ham and Barry's tea and Kimberley biscuits. It was very special.

As I stood in that windswept car park, I exchanged a few words with a brave father and son from Donegal who were setting off in their waterproofs and carrying their sticks. I got back in the car for a few minutes to eat a sandwich, figuring that if I ever made it to the top, it would be too cold and wet to sit and eat. I eventually started walking and passed another ominous sign and one which I didn't remember having seen before. It was a notice from the Mayo Mountain Rescue pleading to pilgrims that if they felt unwell on the way up, they were to come straight back down! There had also been a large notice board declaring that 'Every pilgrim who ascends the mountain on St Patrick's Day or within the octave or anytime during the months of June, July, August and September and prays in or near the chapel for the intentions of our Holy Father the Pope may gain plenary indulgences on condition of going to confession and holy communion on the summit or within the week.' Those indulgences again! Even though I had no idea what the intentions of the Pope were, I was certainly going to be praying at the top. It was also the month of July and I was even, to my pleasant surprise, going to get holy communion on the summit!

I soon got into my pace and caught up with the Donegal pair who were chatting with a man called Michael. He was also from Donegal and part of a group of thirty-three who had travelled from his parish by coach. It was an annual event for them and the group included a priest who was to say a Mass in the little chapel at the top. I asked Michael what brought him back year after year and he said word for word what Pádraig had told me: "There's just something about it." He added, "I like mountains but there's something holy about this one; all the people walking up it year after year." Michael also happened to mention the BBC series broadcast every year around Easter that shows a group of celebrities of all faiths and none walking to a sacred place. I was struck that he also used the word transformation to describe the process that some of those people undergo.

By some miracle the rain had stopped and when I turned round I was rewarded with views over Clew Bay that were as clear and as incredible as the two times I'd been there before. There was a new spring in my step as I passed more and more of the Donegal gang. They varied in age from five girls in their teens to a man in his eighties. And it was the latter who seemed to be getting up the quickest, certainly more so than his daughter who was struggling a bit. I had some lovely exchanges with several of the group. The path has been made gradually easier over the years and after an hour and a quarter I spotted the little white chapel and I was there on the top again. I arrived at the same time as a woman who informed me with great excitement that it was her first time at the age of sixty-nine despite being born in Mayo and living for many years in Galway. When I asked why she'd decided to climb it now she replied that it was on her bucket list of things to do before she turned seventy in three months' time! She was there with her two daughters. The next woman I spoke to was also there for the first time and she was doing it to remember her brother who, sadly, had died an alcoholic. She clearly felt some responsibility for what had happened to him and I suppose that she was one of those who would be walking in a spirit of penitence.

Over the next hour I sat at the top in what was now sunshine as the Donegal contingent arrived in dribs and drabs. When all were there, the priest opened up the chapel and we went in. It was a bit rough and ready and some of the rain had got in, which prompted the priest to remark with a smile, "Well it's not the Sistine Chapel!" It really didn't need to be. We stood around the altar and it was one of the most enjoyable and prayerful Masses I've ever attended. The priest had said at the beginning, "We arrive here at this the highest and the holiest point in Ireland and we come with our struggles and our joys." We finished with a spontaneous verse of 'Hail Glorious St Patrick,' and then I thanked the priest. I said I'd always thought it would be special to go to a Mass at the top and that it had been special indeed. I left the group to their photo session and made a fairly hasty descent, getting back to the car park just in time to miss another downpour.

A little later I received a message from a Carlow woman, Claire who has on a few occasions walked part of the way up The Reek. She had told me once of how her father used to say to them as they were struggling up the steep incline, "Be grateful that you're not the women from Kiltimagh!" It was clear that therein lay a story...

...PILGRIMS' TALES...

Women of the Mountain in Hope

My husband John is from Kiltimagh. He lived there as a boy but has lived the past sixty-five years in London. His mother Della and grandmother were Kiltimagh women. His love and memories of Mayo run deep and strong and it is fair to say they have carried him. Della passed onto her firstborn of ten children a connection with the landscape, an awareness of the changing seasons, and an anticipation of what those changes would bring, together with the history and the folklore. They shared a great love of stories and poetry.

I was reminded of one such story recently when Eddie mentioned he was heading off to Mayo to climb The Reek. In earlier times, a pilgrimage there was held on St Patrick's feast day, March 17th. Nowadays, many ascend on the last Sunday in July, the last Sunday before Lughnasa. This particular story has undoubtedly influenced my interest in the history of Irish women: their lives, often overshadowed; and their resolve and ability to have a standing, driven from some inner strength.

I have been spellbound as John tells the story of the women of Sliabh Cairn who walked every year past his bungalow and on through Kiltimagh on their way to Croagh Patrick. Our children have been reminded, when complaining of being too tired to continue with a walk or some task, how these women, some elderly, made this annual pilgrimage. They walked sometimes in small groups, sometimes alone. They were dressed for all weathers, for you can always expect a shower or two in the West of Ireland. When they reached Murrisk they faced a three-to-four-hour hike to the summit. It is a tough 764 metre climb to the top where a little church stands. There would be Mass and Confessions or maybe the Stations. Some would do it barefoot. Some would fast. There could be indulgences gained.

Waving to John and bidding him *Dia dhuit*, God to you, the women would be carrying a bag; probably homemade, maybe sackcloth. They surely would have baked some soda bread, taken a slick of butter, maybe home churned. Perhaps a boiled egg or a slice of bacon thrown in. Each woman would, of course, have left enough food prepared for whoever was left at home. She would have done all her jobs. Made sure the turf or wood was handy for whoever was keeping the home fire burning in her absence. Who would milk the cow? Feed the chickens?

One would be a widow. She would have reared a family, and some or all would have gone to England or America. Maybe one was in Dublin or Galway and came home and gave her the freedom to make this pilgrimage. This day is important to her. Her mother before her has done it. Some of her neighbours are doing it. There is a connection, a community. It is spiritual and very personal. She has made all the preparations, with nothing neglected. It is now her time. Close the gate, send the dog back home, and hit the road.

The great Irish poet Eavan Boland often wrote about Irish national identity and women. In her poems we see her appreciation for the ordinary in life: 'Dailiness' as I heard her call it. Boland died in 2020. Two years before her death she wrote:

Our future will become the past of other women
Show me your hand, I see our past,
Your palm roughened by heat, by frost.
By pulling a crop out of the earth,
By lifting a cauldron off the hearth.

I believe these formidable women walked from their homes to Croagh Patrick and then climbed The Reek, prayed, made the descent and walked home, about a 60-mile round trip, filled with hope. They hoped and prayed that they would complete their pilgrimage; that all would be well at home in their absence; that their family who could not join them would maybe make it the next time to share this special walk, to chat along the road, to be greeted by neighbours and friends en route, to tell and retell some stories. And surely to share forever the memory of that view from the summit across Clew Bay and its 365 emerald Islands.

Claire, Ireland

Shortly before that third ascent of mine I had written to Claire and I explained that I was just about to set off but that the weather wasn't great. There was a most uplifting message from her awaiting me on my return: "Oh to be in Clew Bay in any weather! Every trip I make to Ireland is like a pilgrimage. My heart motivates and carries me while my soul sustains me as I navigate the emotions that envelop me until I am back in Islington and have the kettle on." She mentioned as well that one of the most enduring memories of her last visit to Croagh Patrick was, "sitting by the National Famine Memorial at Murrisk. Looking out across the Bay. The beauty, the tranquillity, the absolute sense of connection with my ancestors. So much resonance. I hope you get to sit there."

I hadn't managed to sit in that spot but I sent a message back to Claire. I told her how at the end of my walk I had stopped at the bottom next to the statue of St Patrick, taken a deep breath and simply said 'thank you': for that incredible day in that incredible place; and so too for my ancestors.

CHAPTER 10

A PILGRIM ON THE WAY

As I'd stood at the bottom of Croagh Patrick and looked up at that holy mountain I'd felt such a deep sense of gratitude. This was a common theme for me as I came to the end of a pilgrimage and it seemed to be as well for many of those beautiful people I had walked with in so many beautiful places. As Alison said about her walks to Rome and elsewhere, "Aren't we lucky," and as Hanne remarked in Santiago, "We're walking for fun!"

The actor Sue Pollard was one of those who took part in the 2023 BBC series of *The Pilgrimage* and she reflected at the end on her experience of being a pilgrim: "It reinforces what I've always believed. It's about positivity, trying to engage with people, and just enjoy the moment. Faith is supposed to be joyful...anything that can help you, and trying to be a better person...that's what I take away from this: positivity, and just do it while you can!"

I wouldn't wish to detract from the experience of those through the ages who have seen pilgrimage as a form of penitence and who may as well have been seeking those infamous indulgences i.e. a cancelling out of earthly sin in the hope of a quicker route to heaven. However, I'll never forget the boyish grin of the priest from Donegal as he celebrated Mass in that damp little chapel at the summit of Croagh Patrick. I'll never forget the way he engaged with his parishioners and how he thanked them all for the fellowship they'd shared during the day, and in particular a man called Kevin who had encouraged him and almost carried him when he thought he wouldn't make it up the steepest section. And I'll never forget the sense of joy amongst that group. I'll also never forget the huge smile on the face of that Mayo-born woman who was there on the top for the first time, just three months shy of her seventieth birthday. As Sue said, just do it while you can!

Another of those walking with Sue Pollard in the 2023 series was a Muslim man Nabil, who said, "The suffering is part of the experience," and I think this is true. Going on foot for long distances over days, weeks or even months is tough. But it also brings people together in a profound way and leads to the most intimate of connections. We find ourselves in an unfamiliar environment and, as Phil McCarthy observes, you don't know who is going to be in the bunk bed next to you that night. You don't even know sometimes whether you're going to get a bed! This makes us more reliant on the kindness of strangers. And it can lead to the most wonderful encounters. There's also something about putting ourselves at the mercy of the unexpected and as a New Zealander friend Chris John observes about the experience of travelling in general: "The odd moments of grace occur; usually when something goes wrong with my plans!"

And going back to those words of Hanne, it can be such great fun! How I have roared with laughter on the Camino in particular with people I had met for a brief moment and in most cases would never meet again: people from different countries and speaking different languages, people from various backgrounds and social milieu. Some walking quickly, some walking slowly; some doing it for religious reasons, some doing it for sport; some having a good day, some having a bad day. All of us together in that little window of time: united by our blisters and by our basic human need of food, shelter, direction and companionship. As I've mentioned already, I was struck too by how many of my fellow pilgrims remarked that they were seeing wildflowers for the first time! We start to notice things, and that was very much the case for the writer John Connell after he left his home in Co. Longford to go on pilgrimage in Co. Kerry.

John had in 2022 been reflecting on a lack of wonder during the preceding year and a half, when, due to the COVID pandemic, every day had felt the same and opportunities for travel had been restricted. In a 'normal' year he would be heading off to Spain to sip a *café con leche* on a beach or spotting coyotes in an American national park. On this occasion he was richly rewarded by his travels closer to home, which was the 'wild and beautiful' west coast of Ireland in order, as he put it 'to recharge my spirits.' He described it as 'a journey into wonder.' Connell argues that human beings need, like the birds, to move around each year, to go 'in search of a new view, a new experience, a new form of wonder.' He certainly found that on the 'Way of the Saint,' an ancient pilgrimage route running from Ventry Beach in the South of the Dingle Peninsula to Mount Brandon in the North. He spotted on the way fifteen different species of rare flowers, one of which is only found on the Dingle Peninsula and on the Iberian Peninsula. He also had an interesting encounter with three apparently stray dogs who become his companions on the trail and, later on, with the farmer who owned them. 'Maybe that's what every pilgrimage is about,' he concluded at the end of a long and tiring but happy day of walking, 'rekindling the wonder of the everyday.'

That has certainly been my experience, and Liis' story In Chapter 4 about the sense of wonder of her daughter reminded me of a precious photo of my daughter and I which was also from a L'Arche Kent pilgrimage. The year was 2001 and Miran was four years old. The photo shows us crouched down together on a promenade along the North Kent coast, with a flint sea wall behind us. We are in rapt concentration as we observe what must have been some tiny insect on the ground. I was incredibly touched years later when I spotted that this picture is the screen saver on Miran's laptop. The photo captures a moment of silent communion between us, and it illustrates the common pilgrimage experience of taking time to stop, and to see.

There's also something attractive about the simplicity of life on the road. You pack your bag in the morning, you put it on your back, and you walk. Yim Soon and I were inspired to walk the Portuguese Coastal Camino after watching YouTube videos of a young man from Manchester called Liam Brown who would pitch his tent each night next to the beach and who said, "Life is simple. And when you keep it simple, you get life!" He declared at the start of the video that he hadn't set out with any religious motivation. He was just enjoying the walking next to the crashing Atlantic waves, having the freedom to sleep wherever he wanted, and to receive with gratitude whatever gifts or encounters were given each day.

Islay is another of the wonderful people I've met while walking. Like Liam, she does not consider herself to be religious. And, like Liam, she has inspired me by her attitude to pilgrimage and to life generally.

...PILGRIMS' TALES...
A Pilgrim on the Way

I didn't set out as a pilgrim. I'd done a fair amount of hiking trips with my family growing up in Canada, and as a young adult had gotten to fit in a lot of walking in many different corners of Europe, but 'pilgrim' always felt a bit too big a word for the likes of me. It connoted a certain depth which I didn't think I deserved. I felt like I was gliding through life as a young twenty-something, living in France with my own beautiful little studio apartment and slew of international visitors. I was a house leader in a L'Arche community where I adored my quirky house mates, felt competent in my job, felt well supported and surrounded by dear friends, had been able to travel extensively, and had already found the love of my life.

Everything was as near perfect as life could get until complications with extending my visa left me with a sudden and unexpected twenty-four hours to leave this life behind, with the additional sting of some government official at the local prefecture saying that I should never have had it in the first place. It was throughout a rushed day of packing up my life and saying my goodbyes that I realized this was not the time to go home to my family in Canada who would be waiting with open arms. I had to find meaning in all of this or I would look back and see this forever as a failure rather than an opportunity.

As I took what I could carry on my back and leaving most of my stuff behind, boarding a night bus from Paris to London in the middle of the night made me feel like the heroine at the beginning of a novel. For the first time in my life my future was a blank slate and I had all the time in the world.

My partner joined me from the Czech Republic and we hiked the Southwest Coast path of England from Lulworth to Sidmouth. It was an exceptionally dry October which permitted us to sleep under the stars every night and live off of salty blackberries until the sight of them made us queasy. Completely unplanned (which for me was a first), we stumbled upon well-loved sites such as Durdle Door and the Jurassic Coast as if we were the first humans on earth to discover them.

I had always thought that in order to be a pilgrim one must be heading towards an ultimate end goal, whether it be a location such as Santiago de Compostela, or the answer to a big philosophical question. I was simply wandering in one direction, knowing that it would lead me one day closer to my future, and that the visible distance along the coast would feel like tangible proof of progress at a point in my life when I was terrified to find myself stuck. And so I spent that fall walking in England, in the Malvern Hills and along the Cotswold Way; walking in Northern Ireland in and around Rostrevor where C.S. Lewis got his inspiration for Narnia. I walked through the chaos of Dublin's port and gritty Glasgow, and I walked across the Isle of Lismore in the Hebrides. I walked until I realized I was a pilgrim on a search for a home intrinsic to me rather than extrinsic. I walked until I saw that I'd always been a pilgrim without realizing it, and I walked until I was at peace with the idea of heading back to the other side of the Atlantic for Christmas and to start my next chapter.

Islay, Canada

Whether we call it a pilgrimage or a long-distance walk, it can be, as Islay and countless others have discovered, a life-changing experience. It takes us out of the ordinary, out of our comfort zones. We have the chance to see things we wouldn't normally see, to meet people we wouldn't normally meet. We discover sometimes the most extraordinary things and then we return to our ordinary lives a little bit changed, a little bit transformed by the experience.

Each of the places mentioned in the chapter titles of this book have had people walking towards them for centuries. Those people have brought their joys and their struggles. As I've said throughout the book, whether the place of destination contains the 'real' relics or presence of a holy person is for me not really that important in the end. What matters is that pilgrims have been walking towards or visiting that recognised holy place day after day, year after year, so that the very stones on the ground seem sacred.

I was staying once in a Buddhist temple in Korea and the head nun asked me over a cup of green tea what made me happy. I thought for a moment and then replied that it was when I felt connected, both with other people and with the natural world. On my various long-distance walks on the Camino and in other places I have experienced the most precious and incredible connections with people and with place. Those people I have journeyed with for a fleeting moment have touched my heart and I hope I may have touched theirs. With our stories and our laughter, and even with our blisters and our tears, it has truly felt at times like another day in paradise.

BIBLIOGRAPHY

Santiago

Brierley, John. *A Pilgrims Guide to the Camino de Santiago* (Forres: Camino Guides, 2015)

Canterbury

Baldwin Martin, Norah. *Canterbury* (London and Glasgow: Blackie & Son Ltd, 1951)

Boyle, John. *The Illustrated Portrait of Canterbury* (London: Robert Hale Ltd, 1988)

Loxton, Howard. *Pilgrimage to Canterbury* (London: David & Charles, 1978)

Ward, H.S. *The Canterbury Pilgrimages* (London: A & C Black, 1904)

Watt, Francis. *Canterbury Pilgrims and their Ways* (London: Methuen & Co Ltd, 1917)

White, Charles. *The Pilgrims' Way* (London General Omnibus Company Ltd, 1915)

Rome

Hughes, Gerard W. *In Search of a Way* (London: Darton, Longman & Todd, 2021)

McCarthy, Phil. *Rome Alone* (2012)

Jerusalem

Dalrymple, William. *From the Holy Mountain* (London: Harper Perennial, 2005)

Dintaman, Anna & Landis, David. *Walking the Jesus Trail* (Harrisonburg, VA, 2017)

Hughes, Gerard W. *Walk to Jerusalem* (London: Darton, Longman & Todd, 1991)

Hughes, Gerard W. *God in all Things* (London: Hodder & Stoughton, 2004)

Stagg, Guy. *The Crossway* (London: Picador, 2018)

Walsingham

Bull, Andy. *London to Walsingham Camino* (Hindhead: Trailblazer Publications, 2022)

Other books by Eddie Gilmore

Looking Ahead with Hope- stores of humanity, wonder and gratitude in a time of uncertainty (London: Darton, Longman & Todd, 2021)

The Universe Provides- finding miracles and inspiration in unexpected places (London: Darton, Longman & Todd, 2023)

Printed in Dunstable, United Kingdom